Alex Haley & Malcolm X's

THE AUTOBIOGRAPHY
OF MALCOLM X

NOTES

A CONTEMPORARY
LITERARY VIEWS BOOK

Edited and with an Introduction by
HAROLD BLOOM

© 1996 by Chelsea House Publishers, a division of Main Line Book Co.

Introduction © 1996 by Harold Bloom

Printed and bound in the United States of America.

First Printing
1 3 5 7 9 8 6 4 2

Cover illustration: UPI/Bettmann

Library of Congress Cataloging-in-Publication Data

The autobiography of Malcolm X / edited and with an introduction by Harold Bloom.
p. cm. — (Bloom's Notes)
Includes bibliographical references (p.) and index.
ISBN 0-7910-4052-6
1. X, Malcolm, 1925–1965. Autobiography of Malcolm X. 2. X, Malcolm, 1925–1965. 3. Black Muslims—Biography. 4. Afro-Americans—Biography. I. Bloom, Harold. II. Series.
BP223.Z8L5716 1995
320'.5'4'092—dc20
[B]
95-45109
CIP
AC

Chelsea House Publishers
1974 Sproul Road, Suite 400
P.O. Box 914
Broomall, PA 19008-0914

Contents

User's Guide

This volume is designed to present biographical, critical, and bibliographical information on Malcolm X, Alex Haley, and *The Autobiography of Malcolm X*. Following Harold Bloom's introduction, there appears a detailed biography of the authors, discussing the major events in their lives and their important literary works. Then follows a thematic and structural analysis of the work, in which significant themes, patterns, and motifs are traced. An annotated list of characters supplies brief information on the chief characters in the work.

A selection of critical extracts, derived from previously published material by leading critics, then follows. The extracts consist of such things as statements by the authors on their work, early reviews of the work, and later evaluations down to the present day. The items are arranged chronologically by date of first publication. A bibliography of Malcolm X's and Haley's writings (including a complete listing of all books they wrote, cowrote, edited, and translated, and selected posthumous publications), a list of additional books and articles on them and on *The Autobiography of Malcolm X,* and an index of themes and ideas conclude the volume.

Harold Bloom is Sterling Professor of the Humanities at Yale University and Henry W. and Albert A. Berg Professor of English at the New York University Graduate School. He is the author of twenty books and the editor of more than thirty anthologies of literature and literary criticism.

Professor Bloom's works include *Shelley's Mythmaking* (1959), *The Visionary Company* (1961), *Blake's Apocalypse* (1963), *Yeats* (1970), *A Map of Misreading* (1975), *Kabbalah and Criticism* (1975), and *Agon: Towards a Theory of Revisionism* (1982). *The Anxiety of Influence* (1973) sets forth Professor Bloom's provocative theory of the literary relationships between the great writers and their predecessors. His most recent books are *The American Religion* (1992) and *The Western Canon* (1994).

Professor Bloom earned his Ph.D. from Yale University in 1955 and has served on the Yale faculty since then. He is a 1985 MacArthur Foundation Award recipient and served as the Charles Eliot Norton Professor of Poetry at Harvard University in 1987–88. He is currently the editor of the Chelsea House series Major Literary Characters and Modern Critical Views, and other Chelsea House series in literary criticism.

Introduction

HAROLD BLOOM

The life and work of Malcolm X cannot be interpreted coherently apart from the history of "the Nation of Islam," an American religion founded in 1930 in black Detroit by the charismatic Wali Fard the Prophet, who asserted he was an Arab. The Honorable Wallace D. Fard Muhammad disappeared in 1934, as mysteriously as he had come, but handed on his movement to the disciple he named Elijah Muhammad. Fard's message was that he had arrived from Mecca in order to return the "so-called negro" to his ancestral faith, Islam. Yet the Nation of Islam or Black Muslims were endowed by Fard with a mythology and doctrines very unlike anything in orthodox Islam, whether Sunni or Shi'ite. Fard, later proclaimed by Elijah Muhammad to have been Allah in disguise, addressed himself only to blacks. Here is Elijah Muhammad's version of Fard's central myth, which is that Yakub, a renegade black of sinister, indeed diabolical genius, created the white race:

> The great archdeceivers (the white race) were taught by their father, Yakub, 6,000 years ago, how to teach that God is a spirit (spook) and not a man. In the grafting of his people (the white race), Mr. Yakub taught his people to contend with us over the reality of God by asking us of the whereabouts of that first One (God) who created the heavens and the earth, and that, Yakub said, we cannot do. Well, we all know that there was a God in the beginning that created all these things and do know that he does not exist today. But we know again that from that God the person of God continued until today in His people, and today a Supreme One (God) has appeared among us with the same infinite wisdom to bring about a complete change.

Fard, the Supreme One or God, postulated Yakub as the Devil, his opposite and enemy, and so the white race, as the creatures of Yakub, are children of the Devil. This was the potent teaching of Fard's protégé, Elijah Muhammad, whose principal disciple was Malcolm X, until he fell away (from the nation of Islam's perspective) or came into his own, in Malcolm's own estimate. Malcolm's wry epitaph for his relationship to Elijah, as phrased in the *Autobiography*, was: "I had

believed in Mr. Muhammad more than he believed in himself."
The final eighty pages of the *Autobiography* trace the process
of development that began when Malcolm decided to think for
himself.

Henceforth Malcolm, like his friend Warith Deen Muhammad,
son of Elijah, was an orthodox Sunni of the American Muslim
Mission, headed by the Imam Warith Deen Muhammad. As
El-Hajj Malik El-Shabazz, Malcolm made his pilgrimage to
Mecca, and experienced the interracial brotherhood of Islam,
not "Christianity's double standard of oppression," as the
Autobiography puts it. The closing pages of the *Autobiography*
are shadowed by Malcolm's premonitions of his impending
murder by the Nation of Islam. The ultimate pathos, approach-
ing a tragic dignity, of the *Autobiography* comes in these
pages, as Malcolm expresses his yearning for study, whether of
African languages, or Chinese, or the law, or "almost any subject you can mention." Malcolm's best epitaph may be one of
the most poignant of all his statements: "I would just like to
study. I mean ranging study, because I have a wide-open
mind." ✤

Biography of
Malcolm X

Malcolm X was born Malcolm Little on May 19, 1925, to Earl and Louise Little in Omaha, Nebraska. Shortly before Malcolm was born, Earl Little was nearly lynched by the Ku Klux Klan for his outspoken advocacy of the Universal Negro Improvement Association, the organization founded by Marcus Garvey to promote black pride and black rights. The Littles left Omaha when Malcolm was a baby and settled in East Lansing, Michigan, where Earl Little continued his activism. In 1931 Malcolm's father was viciously beaten and run over by a trolley car, and his killers—most likely a white mob—were never brought to justice.

Devastated by this tragedy, the Little family struggled to survive. Louise Little managed to support her children on welfare until 1937, when she suffered a mental breakdown. Malcolm was placed with a white foster family but soon ended up in a juvenile detention center. Although he was a good student—in junior high school, he was elected class president by his mostly white classmates—he dropped out of school after the eighth grade and joined his half sister in Boston.

As a young shoe shiner at the lively Roseland State Ballroom, Malcolm became involved in dancing, drinking, gambling, and hustling. In late 1941, he moved to New York City and joined the Harlem underworld of drug dealers, numbers runners, and armed robbers. Eventually he moved back to Boston, where he was arrested for burglary in 1946 and sentenced to ten years in prison.

While in prison, Malcolm experienced a profound conversion. At the encouragement of some of his siblings and a few of his fellow prisoners, he began to study the doctrine of the Nation of Islam, a Black Muslim religious sect. Elijah Muhammad, the head of the Nation, preached a message of black separatism and resistance to white oppression. Remembering his own father's activism, Malcolm converted to the faith and dropped his surname—which had been given to his ancestors by white Christian slaveholders—in favor of the letter *X*.

After his release from prison in 1952, Malcolm X plunged wholeheartedly into the black rights movement, disseminating the Nation's teachings "to stir and wake and resurrect the black man." In marked contrast to southern civil rights leaders such as Martin Luther King, Jr., Malcolm X disdained nonviolence and urged blacks to use "any means necessary" to combat racism. Delivering spellbinding speeches on street corners and in neighborhood gathering places throughout the nation's urban areas, he attracted thousands of followers and organized many new temples. In 1954, Elijah Muhammad rewarded him by appointing him the head of Harlem's Temple Number Seven.

Malcolm X worked tirelessly to advance the Nation of Islam, and his impassioned speeches earned him great notoriety. Though he deferred to Elijah Muhammad's authority, he was designated as the Nation's public representative in 1962. Alex Haley reported on Malcolm X and the Black Muslims for national publications such as *Reader's Digest* and *Playboy* and was approached by a publisher in 1963 to write an "as told to" autobiography of the dynamic leader. Malcolm X agreed to the book and met periodically with Haley over the next two years.

As his fame grew, Malcolm X drew increasing criticism from both whites and blacks. Many whites were alarmed by his militant assertion that only radical techniques could solve America's racial problems. Other Black Muslims, jealous of Malcolm X's influence, convinced Elijah Muhammad that his protégé was stealing his power. In November 1963, citing a negative comment Malcolm X made about the Kennedy assassination, Muhammad suspended him for ninety days.

Hearing rumors that a high-ranking Black Muslim had ordered him killed, Malcolm X left the Nation of Islam in March 1964 and created Muslim Mosque, Incorporated. Soon after, he journeyed to Africa and the Middle East, making a spiritual pilgrimage to Mecca, the Islamic holy city. Immersed in the Islamic world, Malcolm X renewed his faith and adopted the Muslim name "El-Hajj Malik El-Shabazz"; welcomed by white

Muslims overseas, he discovered that black supremacy was not a tenet of traditional Islam and realized that not all whites were the "devils" he had proclaimed them to be. When he returned to the United States in May 1964, Malcolm X founded the Organization of Afro-American Unity, a secular group that aimed to promote black nationalism worldwide. Though still militant, he exhibited more willingness to work with other civil rights groups.

While Malcolm X's views were evolving rapidly, resistance to him remained firm. Mounting death threats prompted him to prepare mentally for the worst; he ended his autobiography by musing, "If I can die having brought any light, having exposed any meaningful truth that will help to destroy the racist cancer that is malignant in the body of America—then, all of the credit is due to Allah. Only the mistakes have been mine." On the night of February 13, 1965, his house was fire-bombed—he, his pregnant wife, Betty, and their four young daughters only narrowly escaped. A week later, on February 21, Malcolm X was giving a speech at Harlem's Audubon Ballroom when three gunmen—allegedly Black Muslims—assassinated him.

Malcolm X was first and foremost a charismatic speaker and leader, not a writer. Yet his words still resonate on paper, thirty years after *The Autobiography of Malcolm X* became a best-seller. Today, collections of his speeches have been published, many biographies and scholarly studies have appeared, and his life has been made the subject of a controversial film, *Malcolm X* (1992), directed by Spike Lee and starring Denzel Washington. Malcolm X's ideas remain provocative and influ-ential, leading him to be revered as one of America's most compelling black activists. ❖

Biography of
Alex Haley

Alexander Palmer Haley was born on August 11, 1921, in Ithaca, New York, where his father, Simon Haley, was a graduate student at Cornell University and his mother, Bertha Palmer Haley, was planning to enter a musical conservatory. After Alex's birth, his parents took a hiatus from their studies and returned to Bertha's hometown of Henning, Tennessee, where they had two more sons. Young Alex was quite close to both his maternal grandparents, Will and Cynthia Palmer. He had a special fondness for his grandmother, who along with her sisters would entertain him by reciting their family's history back to the first family member to arrive in America from Africa.

Bertha Haley was never in good health and died when Alex was ten. Two years after her death, Haley's father married Zeona Hatcher, and the couple had a daughter. Although Haley did well in school, graduating from high school at age fifteen and then completing two years of college, his youth and his degenerating relationship with his father impelled him to drop out of college and join the Coast Guard. During his twenty years in the Coast Guard, Haley honed his writing skills, first as a ghostwriter of love letters for fellow shipmates and then as a public relations officer in New York and San Francisco. He began to sell stories (usually about the Coast Guard) to men's adventure magazines and in 1954 sold an article to *Reader's Digest*.

Haley took early retirement from the Coast Guard in 1959 and became a writer. Continuing his work for *Reader's Digest*, in 1960 Haley conducted the first of what would be many interviews with a controversial minister of the Nation of Islam named Malcolm X. His reputation as a journalist continued to grow as he conducted a widely read series of interviews with prominent black Americans for *Playboy*. In early 1963, Haley began to interview Malcolm X for *The Autobiography of Malcolm X*, published in 1965. Despite Malcolm X's initial distrust of his interviewer, respect and confidence eventually developed between the two men, and the book remains important both as a personal history of the militant preacher (who was assassinated two weeks after the completion of the manuscript) and as a powerful influence on the civil rights movement.

Haley began research for the book that was to become *Roots* in the early 1960s, envisioning it as a much smaller project that would tell of his family's rise from slavery in the United States. The project quickly expanded, however, and Haley spent more than a decade researching his family's history in the United States, Europe, and Africa. The resulting book (completed ten years after the publisher's deadline) was published in 1976 and became an instant best-seller as well as a critical success. Haley won a special Pulitzer Prize in 1977, the same year that the television miniseries "Roots: The Triumph of an American Family" was aired. The miniseries remains one of the most-watched television shows in the United States and was followed the next year by "Roots: The Next Generation." *Roots* was not without controversy, however. Various sources criticized Haley's scholarship, and more damagingly, the novelist Harold Courlander took Haley to court on charges of plagiarism (Haley settled against the advice of his publishers).

The success of *Roots* resulted in both wealth and celebrity for Haley. Unfortunately, the resulting demands on his time and energy effectively ended his career as a writer. He published a Christmas story, *A Different Kind of Christmas*, in 1988, but produced no more books during his lifetime. He began research into the family history of his paternal grandmother, exploring his family's Irish roots, but died suddenly of a heart attack on February 10, 1992, before completing the project. The book was assembled and in part written by David Stevens and published posthumously in 1993 as *Queen*. ✤

Thematic and Structural Analysis

Chapter one of *The Autobiography of Malcolm X* establishes the dominant theme of Malcolm X's life—the struggle against racism—with its very first sentence, which describes his mother, while pregnant with him, facing harassment by the Ku Klux Klan. Indeed, in relating his father's lifetime of protest (his father, the Reverend Earl Little, a Baptist preacher and an outspoken advocate of Marcus Garvey's Back to Africa movement, "was not a frightened Negro") and his violent death, Malcolm X foreshadows much of his own life.

Although there had been tensions between his father and mother, after the Reverend Little was murdered life in Malcolm Little's Lansing, Michigan, home became truly stressful. Poverty, racism, and intrusive government welfare workers induced a "kind of psychological deterioration [that] hit [the] family circle and began to eat away [their] pride." The eight children "watched [their] anchor giving way" as their mother suffered a breakdown and was sent to a state mental hospital (where she remained for the next twenty-six years); the children were sent to different foster homes. Malcolm X traced much of his anger at white society back to this time when his family was broken apart.

In **chapter two,** Malcolm comes into close contact with whites and witnesses both their good intentions and their prejudices. The state sent the thirteen-year-old to a detention home, where he became a "mascot" for the whites in charge, who treated him with a "kindly condescension." Popular as a "novelty" at his all-white junior high school, he was elected class president and excelled academically.

However, his favorite teacher disillusioned the top student by telling him his race prevented him from becoming a lawyer. This negativity instead spurred Malcolm on to prove himself; in hindsight, he even thanked Allah for the incident, speculating that had he been encouraged to be a lawyer he would have ended up a complacent member of the city's black bourgeoisie. Feeling an increasing "restlessness with being around white people," Malcolm moved to Boston's thriving black community to live with his half-sister Ella. To him, this was the first turning point in his life: "no physical move in my life has been more pivotal or profound in its repercussions."

Chapters three and four detail his coming-of-age adventures in Boston. Exploring the Roxbury neighborhood, Malcolm discovered black families living "high-class" lives but felt "more relaxed among Negroes who were being their natural selves and not putting on airs." Initially he acted like a "hick," but he soon met a friend named Shorty who promised to "school [him] to the happenings." Nicknamed Red for his hair, Malcolm adopted the colorful slang and showy zoot suit style of the "hipsters." After he replaced the Roseland State Ballroom shoeshine boy, who taught him that "everything in the world is a hustle," he gained exposure to music, drinking, drugs, and gambling.

Throughout the book, the chronological account of his life is briefly interrupted by reflections from his more mature perspective, and his interjections express particular dismay at one of his actions during this time: straightening, or conking, his hair with lye. After describing how excited he was by his first conk, he concluded, "How ridiculous I was! . . . This was my first really big step toward self-degradation . . . literally burning my flesh to have it look like a white man's hair." In other ways, though, he remembered becoming more in touch with his blackness. At the "groovy, frantic" dances, his "long-suppressed African instincts broke through, and loose." Exhilarated, he bided his time during the day working as a soda fountain clerk, anxiously awaiting the nights when he could dance and go out with his white girlfriend.

Malcolm broadens his horizons even further in **chapter five,** traveling from Boston to Harlem every other day selling sandwiches on the railroad. "Mesmerized" by the "technicolor bazaar," he considered Harlem "Seventh Heaven" and enthusiastically soaked up the atmosphere. After being fired from the railroads for unruly behavior, he visited Lansing, impressing everyone with his "sharp" style. In Harlem terms, though, he still lacked some sophistication, and as a waiter in a bar he would "have long talks—absorbing everything—with the real old-timers, who had been around Harlem since Negroes first came there." Besides learning the local black history, Malcolm's education included inside tips from the hustlers, pimps, and robbers who frequented the place.

Chapter six depicts the way Detroit Red lived by his wits to make it on the streets of Harlem. In the ghetto, "practically everyone played" the numbers every day, dreaming of a "big hit," so a numbers runner made quite a living. Little value was placed on scruples in this dog-eat-dog world. Malcolm X explained, "In the ghettoes the white man has built for us, he has forced us not to aspire to greater things, but to view everyday living as *survival*—and in that kind of a community, survival is what is respected." He associated with such common criminals as Sammy the Pimp, Dollarbill, and Jumpsteady and picked up the tricks of hustling, trusting no one and learning to spot undercover police.

From hustling he branched out into the lucrative drug market. Socializing with musicians, he "sold reefers like a wild man" and made a lot of money. Initially the lifestyle thrilled him and he "felt, for the first time in [his] life, that great feeling of *free!*" Soon, however, he began to carry a .25 automatic. When the Harlem narcotics squad started trailing him too much, he had to skip out of town, using his old railroad pass to travel with bands who would buy his drugs.

In recounting this time and place, Malcolm X revealed his troubling attitude toward women, which perhaps sprung partially from his problematic relationship with his mother. While he befriended many prostitutes in the neighborhood, he admitted to being "very distrustful of most women." Expecting women to be naturally "fragile and weak," he blamed "domineering, complaining, demanding wives who had just about psychologically castrated their husbands" for the demand for prostitution.

While suspicious of women, Malcolm X was downright "scared" of being drafted into the army. When he was finally summoned by the draft board in 1943, he wore his wildest zoot suit to the induction center and told the army psychiatrist, "I want to get sent down South . . . and kill up crackers!" He was immediately dismissed as 4-F, once again using his wits to survive.

Despite his intelligence, Malcolm X sinks deeper into the desperate criminal world in **chapters seven and eight.** He was "a true hustler—uneducated, unskilled at anything honorable, and . . . exploiting any prey that presented itself." Becoming more of a predator in the "ghetto jungle," he got a bigger gun and committed robberies and stickups in nearby cities. He stole when he needed the money and occupied the rest of his time by gambling, getting high (now on cocaine), dancing, and going to movies. During this time he was often sick, was "mentally dead," and "stayed so high that [he] was in a dream world."

Viewing the dark underbelly of society in this way shaped his pessimistic view of the nation. As a "steerer" for a madam, escorting powerful upper-class whites to black prostitutes, he witnessed firsthand "the hypocritical white man [who] will talk about the Negro's 'low morals.'" Through running numbers and transporting bootleg liquor, he gained some exposure to the Mafia and concluded from the rampant corruption that "in the country's entire social, political and economic structure, the criminal, the law, and the politicians were actually inseparable partners."

At the time, though, he was under the influence of too many drugs to see life clearly. Nearly always high, he became more reckless and had several close calls with danger. In one bold robbery, his friend Sammy the Pimp was grazed by a security guard's bullet. Red also felt the heat from crimes committed by a masked man who fit his rough physical description. In his closest call, he got into a showdown with the dangerous numbers runner West Indian Archie over a money dispute and issues of "face" and "honor" in the hustlers' code. Shorty rushed down from Boston to get him out of town, but Malcolm X just narrowly escaped having to kill or be killed: "Sometimes, recalling all of this, I don't know, to tell the truth, how I am alive to tell it today."

In **chapter nine,** Malcolm X's life of dissipation and crime finally leads him to a moment of reckoning. In Boston, he alarmed his sister and Shorty by behaving "like a predatory animal" who was always high and "wore [his] guns as today [he] wear[s] [his] neckties." After laying low for awhile, he returned to hustling and organized a burglary ring with Shorty, another friend, his longtime white girlfriend, and her sister. To impress the group as a fearless leader, he played Russian roulette saying, "I'm doing this, showing you I'm not afraid to die. Never cross a man not afraid to die." Malcolm X did nearly die twice, though, and felt that only Allah had saved him: once when his white girlfriend's husband came looking for him with a gun and again when he was cornered by police detectives.

Arrested for a burglary, Malcolm and Shorty discovered that their most outrageous "crime" had been consorting with white women. At the end of the chapter, Malcolm X reviewed this portion of his life, explaining that he related the sordid details not to "titillate some readers" but to shed light on the sum total of his experiences, on how he became the person he is. With these remarks, he concluded the first chapter of his life and hinted at the dramatic life-altering transformation to come.

At the opening of **chapter ten,** in February 1946, Malcolm X begins serving his ten-year prison sentence. In his first year, he raged at being behind bars and continued to get high from smuggled drugs. Nicknamed Satan for his atheism, he "would pace for hours like a caged leopard, viciously cursing . . . the Bible and God." The next year, though, he was inspired by a fellow inmate to take a correspondence course to improve his writing and speaking abilities.

His family also offered valuable support. His sister Ella orchestrated his transfer to an experimental rehabilitation jail in Norfolk, Massachusetts, a place with fewer rules and more intellectual stimulation. His brothers and sisters in Detroit wrote him frequently about their conversion to the Nation of Islam and the "Honorable Elijah Muhammad." While Malcolm X initially scoffed at religion, he gave up cigarettes and pork at his favorite brother Reginald's request. Reginald visited the jail to tell his brother more about how history had been "whitened" by white "devils" and the black man had been "brainwashed for hundreds of years." Their talks left Malcolm X greatly unsettled—almost unable to eat—and deeply thoughtful: "It was as though all of that life [in the ghetto jungle] merely was back there, without any remaining effect, or influence." With his siblings' help, he recognized the sinfulness of his past, meditated upon the truth, and considered writing Elijah Muhammad for further guidance.

Although this religious awakening was described as very powerful, Malcolm X inserted some of the distance between himself and the Nation that developed later. He set apart some of the beliefs he adopted by prefacing many statements with "Mr. Elijah Muhammad teaches." After presenting the religious "demonology" of "Yacub's History," which tells of the creation of white devils, he undermined it by explaining that he later learned such tales "infuriated the Muslims of the East," who unfortunately had "left a vacuum into which any religious faker could step and mislead our people." Once again the viewpoint shifts from the account of the original episode to the critical attitude informed by his later experience.

Chapter eleven centers around how Malcolm X truly came to be "saved." He wrote to Elijah Muhammad, who sent him money and words of encouragement, welcoming him into the "true knowledge." In the process of conversion, though, Malcolm X did have to overcome certain trials. He struggled to apply his new beliefs by praying: "For evil to bend its knees, admitting its guilt, to implore the forgiveness of God, is the hardest thing in the world." A more personal obstacle to adopting the new faith arose when his brother Reginald was suspended from the Nation of Islam by Elijah Muhammad for having "improper relations" with a temple secretary. In torment over his brother's rift with the Nation, Malcolm X received a vision (of a man who turned out to resemble Nation founder W. D. Fard) and decided to support Elijah Muhammad. Only in hindsight could he realize that the chastisement would partially be responsible for Reginald's institutionalization and that Muhammad himself would later be accused of the transgressions he condemned Reginald for.

Firmly committed to his religion, Malcolm X also metamorphosed intellectually and politically. His "previous life's thinking pattern slid away . . . like snow off a roof" and a crusader like his father emerged. After copying the whole dictionary by hand to improve his vocabulary, he devoured books of philosophy and history. As "book after book showed . . . how the white man had brought upon the world's black, brown, red, and yellow peoples every variety of the sufferings of exploitation," he wholeheartedly "made up [his] mind to devote the rest of [his] life to telling the white man about himself—or die." In weekly prison debates—his "baptism into public speaking"—he disseminated his growing knowledge and recruited more inmates for the Nation.

Malcolm X begins his new life in **chapter twelve,** after being released from prison in 1952. Moving in with his brother Wilfred's family, he joined Detroit's practicing Muslim community. Wilfred and he worked at a Jewish-owned furniture store, where he "watched brothers entwining themselves in the economic clutches of the white man." Inspired in the Muslim temple by the atmosphere "among black people who had learned to be proud they were black," Malcolm X felt impatient to go out into the streets and spread the message.

Malcolm X received the message directly from Elijah Muhammad. Traveling to Chicago to meet Muhammad for the first time, he "experienced tinglings up [his] spine as [he] never had since." Officially accepted by Muhammad as a member, he became Malcolm X, replacing "the white slavemaster name of 'Little' which some blue-eyed devil . . . had imposed upon [his] paternal forebears." The chapter takes on a hagiographic tone describing the time he spent soaking up Muhammad's wisdom and learning the Nation's history. When not working in a factory job, Malcolm X went "fishing" for converts in "ghetto bars, in the poolrooms, and on the corners" and helped triple the Detroit membership within months. Muhammad sensed his potential, and within a year Malcolm X was appointed assistant minister of Temple Number One.

The seeds of future conflicts had already been planted, though. The Federal Bureau of Investigation (FBI) surveillance of Malcolm X evidently had begun, as he was confronted by an FBI agent about not registering for the Korean War draft. (He then registered as a Muslim conscientious objector and was never called.) While he reminisced about his influential, emotional connection to Elijah Muhammad, the mood was inevitably tainted by their later rift. He regretfully concluded,

"Mr. Muhammad and I are not together today only because of envy and jealousy. I had more faith in Elijah Muhammad than I could ever have in any other man upon this earth." While not listing any specific problems in this early period, he hinted at the "psychological and spiritual crisis" that lay ahead—an illustration of the constant tension between writing the story of his life while continuing to live that life and change his perspectives.

In **chapter thirteen,** Malcolm X really settles into his life as a Muslim. Feeling "ever more awed" by Muhammad, he quit his Ford Motors factory job to devote his service to the "little humble lamb of a man." After opening new temples in Boston and Philadelphia, Malcolm X was named the minister of New York City's Temple Seven. Upon returning to Harlem after nine years, he found many of his old friends were dead and many more destitute, allowing him to see clearly the "pitiful" existence he had escaped thanks to Allah. The strict Muslim moral code—which prohibited eating pork, smoking, drinking, dancing, gambling, and dating among other things—inhibited many Harlemites from joining, but Malcolm X remained determined.

When he started out, "one bus couldn't have been filled with the Muslims in New York City," but he continually passed out leaflets, worked the crowds already gathered at Black Nationalist meetings, and spoke to the masses letting out of Christian church services. He shrewdly "tailored the teachings" to emphasize their appeal to different groups. As his Harlem congregation grew, he also helped launch temples in Hartford, Connecticut, Springfield, Massachusetts, and even Atlanta, Georgia. Muhammad would sometimes "chastise" him, reminding him to have patience and not push so hard.

His "total commitment to Islam," combined with his negative view of women, made Malcolm X in no rush to get married. Judging women by his past experiences, he deemed them "only tricky, deceitful, untrustworthy flesh," who often "ruined, or at least tied down" men. Indeed, some women complained to Muhammad that Malcolm X was unfair when he preached about the differences between men and women. He stubbornly maintained, "While a man must at all times respect his woman, at the same time he needs to understand that he must control her if he expects to get her respect." Evidencing one of his blind spots, Malcolm X did not recognize how his patronizing, disparaging attitude toward women resembled the condescension whites expressed to blacks.

In 1956, though, one woman broke through his blinders and attracted his attention. Betty X, a nursing student originally from Detroit, joined Temple Seven and taught classes for the women of the temple. Although acknowledging that he was "halfway impressed by her intelligence" and that she was the "right height . . . and age," Malcolm X was "shocked" to realize he was starting to think of marriage. After receiving Muhammad's approval, he phoned Betty out of the blue and asked her to fly out to Detroit and marry him. With no talk of romance or love—that "Hollywood stuff"—they were married by a Lansing, Michigan, justice of the peace in January 1958.

The couple settled in Queens and remained active in Harlem's Muslim community. Within six years, the couple had four daughters, and Malcolm X grudgingly admitted, "I guess by now I will say I love Betty. . . . she's one of the very few— four women—whom I have ever trusted." He did not allow family life to distract him, though, and was rarely at home: "Awakening this brainwashed black man and telling this arrogant, devilish white man the truth about himself, Betty understands, is a full-time job." Shortly after his marriage, that full-time job brought him greater notoriety: after fifty Fruit of Islam men peacefully protested to ensure that a Black Muslim brutalized by police received proper medical treatment, both Harlem's police and black community took notice.

In **chapters fourteen and fifteen,** Malcolm X and the Nation of Islam take the spotlight. Malcolm X founded a Muslim newspaper, *Muhammad Speaks,* and also wrote columns for papers in Harlem and Los Angeles. Press coverage of the growing movement exploded in late 1959, with the television documentary "The Hate That Hate Produced" and the publication of C. Eric Lincoln's book *The Black Muslims in America.* The TV exposé, full of "shocker" images, outraged the public and unleashed a torrent of accusations of "reverse racism" from both whites and blacks.

Much of the attention was focused on the articulate, outspoken Malcolm X, and he was invited to numerous panel discussions and debates around the country. Disgusted by the racism and hypocrisy of his critics—especially the "trained black puppets" who supported the white man—he would "pour on pure fire in return." Never shying away from controversy, he preached to blacks that the only way they would be "saved is not to *integrate* into this corrupt society, but to *separate* from it, to a land of our *own,* where we can reform ourselves." Although he knew it would be "foolish to let the white man maneuver [him] against the civil rights movement," he often made disparaging remarks about the nonviolent movement and its latest "civil rights 'advance.'" In his opinion, the northern Freedom Riders should have worked on the problems in their own backyard rather than go down South, and the March on Washington—which he nicknamed the "Farce on Washington"—degenerated into an integrated "picnic" instead of an effective protest by "angry revolutionists."

This period of growth was one of the best times in Malcolm X's life. The temples, now called mosques, continued to expand as more middle-class blacks embraced the Nation's message of black self-pride and economic self-determination. Introducing Elijah Muhammad at mass rallies, he would reach some of his "life's peaks of emotion." When his asthma worsened in 1961, Muhammad moved to Arizona and designated Malcolm X his representative. While speaking at Harvard Law School, Malcolm X had an epiphany about his life and his religion. Looking out the window at the area where his burglary gang had been headquartered, images of his past life "rocked [him] like a tidal wave." He humbly vowed that he "never would forget that any wings [he] wore had been put on by the religion of Islam."

Chapter sixteen details another milestone in Malcolm X's life, his rift with the Nation of Islam. He admitted that he had questioned the organization before: "I thought privately that we should have amended, or relaxed, our general non-engagement policy. . . . In the Little Rocks and the Birminghams and other places, militantly disciplined Muslims should also be there." However, he had always yielded to Elijah

Muhammad, the Nation's spiritual "beacon." As early as 1955, he had heard rumors of Muhammad's infidelity, but he had refused to believe "anything as insane-sounding." When the truth became clear—Muhammad faced two paternity suits from former secretaries—Malcolm X tried to shield Muhammad and find biblical prophecy to explain the wrongs he had committed.

Muhammad disregarded Malcolm X's loyalty and distanced him from the organization. Jealous Muslims accused Malcolm X of "playing 'coast-to-coast Mr. Big Shot,'" and the newspaper that he had founded refused to give him any coverage. In 1963 Muhammad used an unsympathetic comment Malcolm X had made about the Kennedy assassination to silence him officially. Soon after, Malcolm X received death threats that he knew could have only been approved by Muhammad. Remembering his painful "psychological divorce" from the Nation, he revealed, "The thing to me worse than death was the betrayal." On his own after twelve years, Malcolm X founded the Muslim Mosque, Inc., an organization working for blacks' human rights, and borrowed money from his sister Ella to make a pilgrimage to the Islamic holy city of Mecca.

Chapters seventeen and eighteen chronicle his evolving spirituality and his discovery of the "true Islam" of orthodox Muslims. His whole pilgrimage, or hajj, was an eye-opening experience, exposing him to Arabic prayers and orthodox rituals for the first time. The sincere, generous hospitality he received caused a sea change in his attitude, leaving him "utterly speechless and spellbound by the graciousness [he saw] displayed all around [him] by people *of all colors.*" He was moved to write a letter home explaining his new awareness of the potential for brotherhood and his intentions to look past skin color to attitudes and actions. This represented another dramatic shift for him, but it still made sense in his life, which he devoted to telling the truth about racial issues: "Even I was myself astounded. But there was precedent in my life for this letter. My whole life had been a chronology of—*changes.*"

Continuing his journey throughout Arabia and Africa, Malcolm X received a warm welcome everywhere. Freed from the yoke of American racism, he displayed a lighthearted joyfulness and a wry sense of humor: while sleeping under the night sky with fellow Muslims of every race and background, he realized that they "all snored in the same language." Prince Faisal of Arabia honored him as a guest of the state, and he associated with many leaders and ambassadors, even addressing the Ghanaian Parliament. After a few months, he returned to America reinvigorated and eager to "develop a working unity [among Afro-Americans and Africans] in the framework of Pan-Africanism."

The **final chapter** sets forth the months before Malcolm X's death and his conclusions about his life. Fully aware "that any moment of any day, or any night, could bring [him] death," he lived with an even greater urgency; he returned to Africa and the Middle East once but spent most of his time launching the secular black nationalist Organization of Afro-American Unity and trying to change his old Black Muslim image. Although he clearly stated his new insight that "not all white people are racists," he continued to unsettle the white press by advocating change "by any means necessary."

Resigned to a violent death, Malcolm X was convinced that he would not be alive when his book was published. Thus, although the whole book had focused on his constantly evolving attitudes and behavior, he adopted a tone of finality here. He reviewed some of his regrets—such as his unmet dream of becoming a lawyer—and predicted more racial unrest and riots until the country's underlying social problems are solved; he also foresaw that his image would be used as a "convenient symbol of 'hatred.'" Expressing a desire to leave a record of his life that may be of some value, he connected his personal story to the greater black experience and wished that "the objective reader, in following [his] life—the life of only one ghetto-created Negro—may gain a better picture and understanding than he has previously had of the black ghettoes which are shaping the lives and the thinking of almost all of the 22 million Negroes who live in America." In the end, he hoped to have made a difference, humbly giving credit to Allah for all the "meaningful truth" he has exposed.

The **epilogue** presents Alex Haley's perspective on collaborating with Malcolm X. He describes how he gradually gained Malcolm X's trust and how he drew him out of his shell by asking about his mother and by leaving napkins on which to scribble offhand comments. Haley gives a relative insider's view, offering glimpses of Malcolm X's private side. Finally, he relates the details Malcolm X could not: his assassination on February 21, 1965, while speaking at Harlem's Audubon Ballroom, the arrest of three Black Muslims for his murder, and the outpouring of public reaction. Tying together the diverse threads of Malcolm X's life—his troubled childhood, his criminal activity, his fiery speeches, his ever-evolving spirituality—Haley concludes that his "electric personality" will be remembered by history. ❖

—Anne M. McDonnell

List of Characters

Malcolm X is the narrator of his life story, relating events forthrightly and reflectively. Born Malcolm Little, he embraces the Muslim faith while in prison for robbery and later adopts the surname X. Once out of jail, he becomes a minister in the Nation of Islam and is the driving force behind the religion's growth into a powerful national organization. After Nation leader Elijah Muhammad betrays him, Malcolm X forms the Muslim Mosque, Inc. An international figure, he travels to the Middle East to study Islam and begins to advocate pan-Africanism, continually evolving his views. (At this time, he changes his name to El-Hajj Malik El-Shabazz.) He is gunned down in 1965 by three men identified as Black Muslims.

Elijah Muhammad is the spiritual leader of the Nation of Islam who takes Malcolm X under his wing. He teaches his loyal, enthusiastic disciple about the Nation's history and theology and appoints him a minister. When Muhammad's asthma worsens, he designates Malcolm X to be his spokesman but soon tries to rein him in as his fame and influence grow. Muhammad violates the tenets of his faith by having affairs and fathering children out of wedlock but maintains his power over the Nation. He tries to silence Malcolm X and orders Black Muslims to kill him.

Betty X is Malcolm X's wife. A nursing student from Detroit, she meets Malcolm X while working as a health teacher at Harlem's Temple Number Seven. One of the few women he trusts, Betty X is a patient wife and a devoted mother to their four daughters.

Ella, the oldest child of Earl Little, is Malcolm X's half sister. Possessing similar temperaments, she and Malcolm X get along well for the most part and admire each other. Ella consistently supports her brother, bringing him to Boston when he is a teenager and later funding his pilgrimage to Mecca when he is a Muslim minister.

Reginald is one of Malcolm X's younger brothers. Reginald leaves the merchant marine to live in Harlem with his brother, who both watches over him and seeks his admiration. The two become very close, and it is at Reginald's urging that Malcolm X gives up cigarettes and pork and converts to Islam. When Reginald is suspended from the Nation of Islam for "improper relations" with women, Malcolm X struggles with his conscience but finally supports Elijah Muhammad. Reginald is devastated by his religious community's censure and is later institutionalized.

Shorty is an aspiring musician who befriends Malcolm X when he first moves to Boston. He helps Malcolm X find a job, teaches him the ways of the neighborhood, and gives him his first conk hairstyle. When Malcolm X gets into serious trouble in Harlem, Shorty rescues him and brings him back to Boston. Shorty helps Malcolm X start a burglary ring and goes to prison after they get caught.

Wilfred, Malcolm X's oldest brother, is one of the people who urges Malcolm X to convert to the Nation of Islam. When Malcolm X is released from prison, Wilfred takes him into his home, finds him a job, and teaches him more about Islam. Wilfred becomes a minister and remains with the Nation even after Malcolm X has broken with the organization.

Sammy the Pimp is Malcolm X's closest friend in Harlem. A pimp and a hustler, Sammy commits robberies with Malcolm X.

Sophia is a blond white woman who starts a romance with Malcolm X in Boston and continues to see him on the side after she marries a white man. She is a member of his burglary ring.

Laura is a shy, intelligent, respectable girl that Malcolm X meets in Boston. Though she is his best lindy-hopping dance partner, Malcolm X dumps her for a white woman. Exposed to the seamy side of Boston by Malcolm X, Laura becomes a "wreck" of a woman, much to his remorse.

Earl Little, Malcolm X's father, is a Baptist minister who advocates the black pride and "Back to Africa" philosophy of Marcus Garvey's Universal Negro Improvement Association (UNIA). A big, tall, tough man with only one eye, he makes an imposing presence and sometimes beats his wife and children. He favors Malcolm—possibly because of his light skin color—and provides a strong example with his fearless outspokenness.

Always a target of white racist groups for his activism, in 1931 he is savagely beaten and left on a streetcar track, where he is run over and killed.

Louise Little is Malcolm X's mother. A West Indian who can "pass" for white, she is ashamed of her white father and tries to prevent light-skinned Malcolm from developing "a sense of color-superiority." An educated woman, she often loses jobs when people learn she is black. After her husband's death, she struggles to support eight children alone and has to go on welfare. She hates accepting charity and talks back to meddling welfare workers. Around 1937, she suffers a breakdown and is institutionalized in a state mental hospital, where she remains for nearly twenty-six years. Malcolm X visits her infrequently and does not like to talk about her.

Alex Haley plays a largely unspoken role, helping Malcolm X to write his memoir. He relates his viewpoints directly in the epilogue. ❖

Critical Views

[Truman Nelson (1911–1987) was an American novelist, historian, and political commentator. Among his
books are *The Torture of Mothers* (1965; on the Harlem
riots of 1964), *The Right of Revolution* (1968), and
biographies of William Lloyd Garrison (1966) and John
Brown (1973). In this review of *The Autobiography of
Malcolm X*, Nelson studies the violence-filled youth of
Malcolm X along with his violent death.]

This is the story of a man struck down on his way to becoming
a revolutionary and a liberator of his people. It is the real
American tragedy: a fall from great heights of promise, not
from inner weakness or self-betrayal, but because assassins
stood up in plain sight, like a firing squad, and put thirteen
shotgun slugs into his chest and bullets in his legs and thighs
as he lay dying.

Malcolm had known the white man's violence from infancy.
Five of his father's six brothers died by violence; one was
lynched, another killed by white police. His father, very strong,
very black, a gun-carrying Baptist minister and a Garveyite
organizer, was killed by having his head bashed in and he was
laid on a car track to be cut in half. The white insurance company called it suicide. When Malcolm, his father's seventh
child, died in Harlem on February 21, 1965, he was accused by
the white press of having "initiated violence."

His mother was nearly white, looked white, but she could
not keep a job when any of her black children showed up, or
her small-town employers found out whose widow she was.
Keeping food on the table and some dignity around it for a
family of eight was an insoluble problem in the 1930s. It drove
her into insanity. The family was broken up, and Malcolm
began a delinquent's progress through the ghettos of Boston
and New York, with conked red hair, a sky-blue zoot suit and
orange knob-toed shoes, all so grotesque on his 6-foot-5 gan-
gling frame that he would stop traffic crossing the street. He

became a hustler, a pimp, a 'narcotics addict' and peddler, a petty thief and armed robber.

The stupendous transformation came while he was serving a ten-year sentence for armed robbery in Massachusetts. He had become the prototype of the hustler, by his own definition: "The hustler out there in the ghetto jungle has less respect for the white power structure than any other Negro in America. He is internally restrained by nothing. To survive he is out there constantly preying on others, probing for any human weakness like a ferret . . . forever frustrated, restless and anxious for some *action*. Whatever he undertakes, he commits himself to it fully, absolutely." ⟨. . .⟩

But the great revelation comes in the Epilogue by his perceptive and enormously skillful amanuensis, Alex Haley. Malcolm was invited to speak in France by a group of African students. He had been talking, in late '64, of the great power of the black and yellow races when seen internationally. I heard him in Harlem, on a platform with Babu, the Zanzibar revolutionary, say the problem is now simply the oppressed against the oppressor. He had begun to renew himself, and his regenerated purpose began to take form, a political form. He was talking now like a member of a revolutionary majority. When he arrived in France, the government banned him as "an undesirable person." He was wrathful and puzzled when he came back to New York.

On Saturday, February 20, he made a most significant phone call to Alex Haley. "I'm going to tell you something, brother. The more I think about what is happening lately, I'm not at all sure it's the Muslims. I know what they can do and what they can't do, and they can't do some of the stuff that's happening to me lately. The more I think of what happened to me in France, I think I'm going to quit saying it's the Muslims. . . . I'm glad that I've been the first to establish official ties between Afro-Americans and our blood brothers in Africa." Then he hung up.

Twenty-four hours later, in the dressing room of the Audubon Ballroom, he said he was going to announce that he had been too hasty in accusing the Muslims because, "things are happening that are bigger than they can do . . . in fact, I'm going to ease some of this tension by telling the black man not to fight himself . . . that it's all part of the white man's big maneuver, to keep us fighting against ourselves." But before he could get this noble resolve on the record, the executioners rose in the first row and the sentence was carried out.

Viewed in its complete historical context, this is indeed a great book. Its dead-level honesty, its passion, its exalted purpose, even its manifold unsolved ambiguities will make it stand as a monument to the most painful of truths: that this country, this people, this Western world has practiced unspeakable cruelty against a race, an individual, who might have made its fraudulent humanism a reality.

—Truman Nelson, "Delinquent's Progress," *Nation,* 8 November 1965, pp. 336, 338

Doris Lessing on the Force of Malcolm X's Personality

[Doris Lessing (b. 1919) spent most of her youth in Southern Rhodesia before emigrating to England and becoming a distinguished novelist. Among her notable works are *The Golden Notebook* (1962) and *Briefing for a Descent into Hell* (1971). In this review of the *Autobiography,* Lessing finds the work unsatisfactory because of Malcolm X's rapidly shifting viewpoints, but she nevertheless finds the force of his personality compelling.]

Malcolm X's autobiography is not an autobiography. A ghost, Alex Haley, made this book—most of it approved by Malcolm X before he died—from speeches, articles, notes of interviews. Against difficulties. Haley is a Negro, but was first regarded by Malcolm X as 'a white man's tool sent to spy'. 'I trust you 70 per cent' was his way of announcing won confidence. Then, the Black Muslim section was done before the break, while Malcolm X was passionately identified with the movement and its leader, Elijah Muhammad. As any politician would, he glossed over the internal difficulties to which he was not deliberately blinding himself. Nor, after the break, could his loyalty to the Negro struggle allow him damaging admissions. So if you want facts about membership, hidden allegiances, military organisation and plans, this book is worthless. Worse: Malcolm X's viewpoint about himself and his ideas shifted during the writing of it. Which brings up again the point recently raised by Truman Capote and his murderers—a relationship between reporter and subject which is bound to be suspicious, resistant, hostile, then overconfiding. Malcolm X was alone, trusted no one, not even his wife, was paranoiac. Like the hero of *Catch-22*, classified as paranoid for believing, a soldier in World War II, that people wanted to kill him.

Haley got nowhere until he carefully depth-bombed: 'I wonder if you'd tell me something about your mother.' 'After that night he never hesitated to tell me the most intimate details of his personal life.' 'It made me face something about myself,' said Malcolm X—and face himself he did, uncovering areas blocked off through misery, drugs, guilt, hate. Malcolm X was not by nature gifted with insight into himself. Learning it came hard. About what he learned he was immediately honest, with the kind of frankness which comes easiest to those who are able to see their lives impersonally, as representative of forces larger than themselves—in his case, the Negro struggle for freedom. His sharply shifting viewpoints about his past would have made this book an unsatisfactory patchwork even if it hadn't used the hypnotic rhetoric of the speeches, the provocative over-simplifications of the polemical writing, as if these were Malcolm X's considered voice. Much better to have had this as straight biography from the shrewd and compassionate Haley. *But,* should we really welcome books like these, where a man in such a prison is opened in trust for the first time to a reporter doing a job? ⟨. . .⟩

Malcolm X came home with a new name, El-Hajj Malik El-Shabbaz (his 'X' had 'replaced the white slavemaster name of "Little" which some blue-eyed devil named Little had imposed upon my paternal forebears'). He came home, too, with considerably modified ideas. With his usual courage, he said so: he was expecting assassination daily. His tactical sense was put to the service of new outlooks. If he had lived, his version of 'The Nation of Islam' would probably have manoeuvred usefully in conjunction with the moderate movements formerly described by him as 'Uncle Tom': as a Black Muslim lieutenant he had chafed because Muhammad would not allow collaboration. He was murdered in 1965 while addressing a meeting in New York.

The Black Muslim sect remains: so does Elijah Muhammad. Its value—apart from its work among ex-prisoners, junkies, prostitutes—has been largely propagandist. The moderate movements, 'the sit-downs, sit-ins and teach-ins', have achieved more in practical terms. If, as the Black Muslims believed, the devil white man can be terrifed by threats of raw violence into parting with his privileges, then Los Angeles would be a better place for its race riots. I gather this is not the case. But what a pity he is dead. He was a most gifted man, and we don't know what he might have become.
> —Doris Lessing, "Allah Be Praised," *New Statesman,* 27 May 1966, pp. 775–76

CHARLES A. HOYT ON MALCOLM X AND THE AMERICAN DREAM

> [Charles A. Hoyt is the author of *Witchcraft* (1981) and the editor of *Minor British Novelists* (1967) and *Minor American Novelists* (1970). In this extract, Hoyt notes that Malcolm X's *Autobiography* reveals how black Americans are robbed of the American dream.]

When we comment upon the disastrous effects of racism upon the Negro family structure, as so many authors have done recently, we should not omit to notice another punishing aspect of the problem: the tendency for blacks to sublimate their distrust and hatred of their own parents—who have failed them—in distrust and hatred of whites. An analyst friend of mine recently told me, "Many of these people have never *seen* a white person until they reach a certain age. What they really find unendurable is the failure of their own parents; and because that is also unexpressible, they visit it upon the whites." This is not a pleasant idea for blacks to grapple with; most of those whom I have approached with it have rejected it with great indignation. It does, however, gain plausibility for a number of Malcolm's utterances.

For example, he told Alex Haley, "I have something to tell you that will surprise you. Ever since we discussed my mother, I've been thinking about her. I realized that I had blocked her out of my mind—it was just too unpleasant to think about her having been twenty-some years in that mental hospital" (*The Autobiography of Malcolm X*, Epilogue). And again, "I have rarely talked to anyone about my mother, for I believe that I am capable of killing a person, without hesitation, who happened to make the wrong kind of remark about my mother."

Perhaps it is necessary to say that there is small comfort for whites in this phenomenon, to whatever extent it may operate. The black who revenges his parents' failure upon the white man is usually not far off the target, since so many of the "failures" are ultimately attributed to a racist society.

Perhaps it was, as Ossie Davis wrote in his beautiful elegy to Malcolm, that he was too much of a man to be a good nigger. For the two things are truly incompatible. One of the most touching moments in the *Autobiography* comes in the epilogue, when Malcolm tells Haley, "I'll never forget the day they elected me the class president. A girl named Audrey Slaugh, whose father owned a car repair shop, nominated me. And a boy named James Cotton seconded the nomination. The teacher asked me to leave the room while the class voted. When I returned I was the class president. I couldn't believe it." When Malcolm said this, he was in his late thirties, and had been describing himself as "the angriest black man in America."

The American dream is still potent; its very strength and beauty, as flashed from a thousand glossy magazines, are the sources of some of the strongest black reactions against it. Because to the black man, it doesn't apply. "Know what they call a black Ph.D. in America?" Malcolm X asks an audience of Negro academicians: "Nigger!" Like the fool in *Lear*, Malcolm X was a pestilent gall to his best friends, ever reminding them of things they would just as soon have forgotten. That was because Malcolm Little, like most blacks who try to play the good part, got what amounted to two basic reactions, no matter how ingenious their variations: contempt, or dismissal.

—Charles A. Hoyt, "The Five Faces of Malcolm X," *Negro American Literature Forum* 4, No. 4 (Winter 1970): 108

CAROL OHMANN ON MALCOLM X AND THE AMERICAN TRADITION

[Carol Ohmann (1929–1989), formerly a professor of English at Wesleyan University, wrote *Ford Madox Ford: From Apprentice to Craftsman* (1964). In this extract, Ohmann argues that *The Autobiography of Malcolm X* is a traditionally American work in the same vein as Benjamin Franklin's autobiography.]

The Autobiography of Malcolm X testifies to the black experience in America. More precisely, it testifies to the personal cost of the black experience in America. The first chapter records the death of Malcolm's father, the victim apparently of whites who resented his propagandizing for Marcus Garvey's back-to-Africa movement; in the "Epilogue," Alex Haley describes the assassination of Malcolm X, shot by three black gunmen on February 21, 1965 as he began to speak in a Harlem ballroom in favor of his Organization of Afro-American Unity. The continuity of experience from first to last in the *Autobiography* is inescapable. The lives of father and son alike were fundamentally shaped to their violent ends by the fact that they were born black in America and tried to combat the inferiority to which their color condemned them.

And yet, at the same time that the *Autobiography* unforgettably tells those of us who do not know it about the black experience, and helps to explain it to those who know it and have yet to understand it—at the same time, the

Autobiography is in many ways a traditionally American work. The evidence of the book itself insists on both its differences from and its similarities to the general American experience. At a time when one hears so often simply that Black is Different (I have just put down a college newspaper in which a black faculty member assures me that as a white I cannot possibly appreciate the aesthetic quality of a certain black drama), it seems to me useful to note some of the ways in which Malcolm X's story, as he told it over a period of two years to Alex Haley, reflects American culture. Despite the fact that Benjamin Franklin could not have bought a bottle of Red Devil lye, and would have had no need or wish to, his *Autobiography* and *The Autobiography of Malcolm X* resemble each other in the conceptions of the self they convey, in the categories by which they apprehend men and events, in the standards by which they judge them, and in the ways, looking backward as autobiographers do, they pattern or structure the raw materials of their own lives. Roughly, what Benjamin Franklin wanted and got for himself and his fellow citizens, Malcolm X also wanted for himself and his people—until in the last year of his life he changed his mind. To put this in a practical academic way, *The Autobiography of Malcolm X* belongs not only in an Afro-American course but in a course in American literature or American autobiography. Both Benjamin Franklin and Malcolm X testify to certain strengths and certain weaknesses in our national ethos, strengths and weaknesses that have characterized us very nearly from, if not from, the beginning.

—Carol Ohmann, "*The Autobiography of Malcolm X:* A Revolutionary Use of the Franklin Tradition," *American Quarterly* 22, No. 2 (pt. 1) (Summer 1970): 131–32

BARRETT JOHN MANDEL ON THE DIDACTIC NATURE OF THE *AUTOBIOGRAPHY*

[Barrett John Mandel (b. 1937) teaches at Rutgers University. He is the editor of *Three Language-Arts*

Curriculum Models (1980). In this extract, Mandel points out that Malcolm X's autobiography is a chronicle of self-learning and also an example for other black Americans.]

The *Autobiography of Malcolm X* is a richly didactic work— didactic in the best sense of the word. As a man who spent the greater part of his life in learning how to be a *human* being, always working toward the goal of humanizing those around him, Malcolm X has written his autobiography in the hagiographical spirit of one who has found hope and even peace and now wishes to help others find them.

Malcolm's recollections carry him from his birth as Malcolm Little on 19 May 1925 to 1965 just before his death as El-Hajj Malik El-Shabazz. Between those two dates, he traces his history. It begins with a nightmarish account of the Ku Klux Klan galloping out of the Omaha night to threaten his father, a Marcus Garvey enthusiast. Malcolm tells of his unhappy boyhood in Michigan where his family was victimized by a racist society's contempt and where on parole from a detention home, he made a success of himself in school by adopting the white man's standards and customs. The autobiography traces Malcolm's descent into the dizzying life of the black underworld of Boston and New York. As "Detroit Red" Malcolm experienced the desperate criminal existence of Harlem, involving himself in narcotics, hustling, and robbery. At last caught by the police and sentenced more for consorting with white women than for burglary, Malcolm is sent to prison. While in jail, he converts to Elijah Muhammad's Nation of Islam, introduced to it and guided by his brother Reginald. From the moment of conversion, Malcolm's life is directed toward personal, spiritual growth, and dedication in his mission to the black world. The Muslim faith could lead all Negroes to a new position of self-respect and dignity. Malcolm traces his ascent in the Nation of Islam ministry until his charismatic power makes him a threat to Elijah Muhammad. Malcolm is forced out of the Muslim Community and so he makes his fateful trip to Mecca and embraces the "true" Muslim faith. He ends his account in the aftermath of his trip to Asia and Africa. Back in New York, he tries, in vain, to fend off the fatal blow which he fears is about to strike him down. At first Malcolm suspects the Black Muslims of wishing his death, but toward the end he has begun to assume that such a plot to cut off his life must be a larger, more sinister affair than that of which the Black Muslims would be capable.

Like St. Augustine, John Bunyan, Jonathan Edwards, and Vavasor Powell, Malcolm has written a spiritual conversion autobiography. The *Autobiography* is that of a sinner who becomes a saint, and the saint, like his Christian parallels, is a preacher. One notices the parallels especially to John Bunyan, who as he became a "saint"—the word was commonly used for puritan bretheren in the seventeenth century and was still used by the Plymouth Bretheren in the nineteenth century—became increasingly repugnant to the established authorities, who went to great lengths to stop his preaching.

Malcolm, trapped in a Manichean world of Evil and Good, is pulled from pole to pole in his slow ascent to self-knowledge. And there are many other parallels to familiar conversion literature. The treatment of sex can serve as an important example. Malcolm tells of his youth spent among pimps and whores. Like the young St. Augustine, Malcolm at first found the good life to be one of fleshly pursuits; his narrative skill goes a long way toward recreating the attractiveness of the early temptations. It is only as the rhythm of his life starts to carry him toward self-regeneration in Islam that he recognizes the need of self-imposed abstinence: "I had always been very careful to stay completely clear of any personal closeness with any of the Muslim sisters. My total commitment to Islam demanded having no other interests, especially, I felt, no women." In *The Autobiography of Malcolm X,* St. Augustine's *Confessions,* Bunyan's *Grace Abounding,* one finds lusty men repressing their physical desires and channeling their energy into their social and spiritual obligations. Sex is vitally, but negatively, important in most spiritual autobiographies; the author's life is to some degree molded by his self-conscious avoidance of sexual intercourse. One's life becomes the phallus.

—Barrett John Mandel, "The Didactic Achievement of Malcolm X's Autobiography," *Afro-American Studies* 2, No. 4 (1972): 269–70

[Ross Miller, a professor of English at the University of Connecticut, has written *American Apocalypse: The Great Fire and the Myth of Chicago* (1990). In this extract, Miller examines the *Autobiography* in the context of early American autobiographical writing, in particular the work of Benjamin Franklin.]

Franklin's personal history, like ⟨Henry⟩ Adams's, is a manikin with which he can study relations. The life of one man becomes the key to mapping the mysteries of the race; and the wonders that are related to the one life are as important as the record of the life itself. Autobiography, at this level, is as much an exercise of will as it is a record of the past.

This posturing, the use of fictions, to get outside of oneself—to be equal to, yet to be more than one is entitled to by birth—is the archetypal pose of the autobiographer. In Malraux's language, it is to identify yourself with no less than the eternal metamorphosis of the earth. In a word, it is that terrible reaching for immortality. Watch Malcolm struggle as he moves to identify himself with the entire black American population. Like the Sultan who dies trying to propagate the earth with his sons and daughters.

> I have given to this book so much of whatever time I have because I feel, and I hope, that if I honestly and fully tell my life's account, read objectively it might prove to be a testimony of some social value. . . .
>
> I think that an objective reader may see how when I heard "The white man is the devil," when I played what had been my own experiences, it was inevitable that I would respond positively; the next twelve years of my life were devoted and dedicated to propagating that phrase among the black people.
>
> I think, I hope, that the objective reader, in following my life—the life of only one ghetto-created Negro—may gain a better picture and understanding than he has previously had of the black ghettoes which are shaping the lives and the thinking of almost all of the 22 million Negroes who live in America.

Malcolm's mythical presence, the pose of an exemplary life, just as Franklin's, is a daring simplification. They are using the autobiography, in part, as a fiction to express personal relationships to history that are true in essence, but are nevertheless suspicious in the exaggerated form they take. The personae of Malcolm and Franklin, in their autobiographies, are bigger than life because they are intended to represent many individuals. The paradox of writing in this mode is that this mythic relationship, although accepted by the writer and his audience, is illusory; it is a literary relation and not a metaphysical one. The fictive aspect of the autobiography is the result of this conflation between a first-person narrator and a naturally third-person persona who share a mutual identity. Malcolm X narrates the history of "Malcolm X," who is simultaneously himself and all black men in America, as Ben Franklin records the story of "Benjamin Franklin," who seems to be all of colonial America. This double identity is not accidental, but is intrinsic to the structure of the autobiography. It is the acting out of the quality William James called the phenomenon of the "twice born." In Franklin's words:

> I should have no objection to a repetition of the same life from its beginning, only asking the advantages authors have in a second edition to correct some faults of the first. So I might, besides correcting the faults, change some sinister accidents and events of it for others more favorable. But though this were denied, I should still accept the offer. Since such a repetition is not to be expected, the next thing most like living one's life over again seems to be a recollection as durable as possible by putting it down in writing.

Franklin could not be clearer. There is that quality to the autobiography that makes writing down the story of a life not so much reliving the past as simply living again.
—Ross Miller, "Autobiography As Fact and Fiction: Franklin, Adams, Malcolm X," *Centennial Review* 16, No. 3 (Summer 1972): 227–28

[Cedric J. Robinson, a professor of political science at the University of California at Santa Barbara, is the author of *Black Marxism: The Making of the Black Radical Tradition* (1983). In this extract, Robinson argues that the collaborative effort of writing *The Autobiography of Malcolm X* can be seen as an extended "psychoanalytic interview" because of the emotional memories that Malcolm had to relive.]

When first approached by Alex Haley (a black free-lance writer) with the idea of writing an autobiography, Malcolm X apparently realized the importance the project might have for everyone but himself. Yet as it evolved he must have come to understand what it was forcing him to acknowledge about himself:

> . . . when something provoked him to exclaim, "These Uncle Toms make me think about how the Prophet Jesus was criticized in his own country!" Malcolm X promptly got up and silently took my notebook, tore out that page and crumpled it and put it into his pocket, and he was considerably subdued during the remainder of that session.

Notwithstanding the cautions of Erikson linked with the unusually "public" nature of Gandhi's work (which was a final compilation of columns written for a newspaper in the form of moral lessons for its readers) in large measure Malcolm X was freely associating in a fashion obviously similar to the non-directive interview familiar to students of Carl Rogers. Haley, frustrated by the unproductiveness of the early "visits," hit upon the stratagem of placing innocent scraps of tissue near Malcolm X since he was an habitual scribbler, writing in abbreviated and short-handed form messages which could not be directly related to the conversational content of his visits. "It was through a clue from one of the scribblings that finally I cast a bait that Malcolm X took."

The relationship, however, between the writer and the "analysand" was cemented for both much later:

> I don't know what gave me the inspiration to say once when he paused for breath, "I wonder if you'd tell me something about your mother?". Abruptly he quit pacing, and the look that he

shot at me made me sense that somehow the chance question had hit him . . . Slowly, Malcolm X began to talk . . . After that night, he never again hesitated to tell me even the most intimate details of his personal life, over the next two years. His talking about his mother triggered something.

It is plain that as Malcolm X remembered his experiences (some of which he claimed he hadn't thought of for years and certainly had never shared with anyone) he relived them. As Malcolm Little (and from this point the appellations will each represent specific psychosocial stages in the man's life) the child, he was "somber to grim." As Detroit Red, the hustler, pimp, dope pusher, burglar and dope "fiend," he was often exuberant:

> One night, suddenly, wildly, he jumped up from his chair and, incredibly, the fearsome black demagogue was scat-singing and popping his fingers, "re-bop-de-bop-blam-blam—". . . And then almost as suddenly, Malcolm X caught himself and sat back down, and for the rest of that session he was decidedly grumpy.

It is thus with a sense of the deep emotional investment involved for the man as well as the force it brought to his reorganizations of his life that the *Autobiography* must be read. As it was being dictated from the Spring of 1963 to the Winter of 1964–65, the man was transisting from the troubled but passionately defensive Muslim minister Malcolm X (who had fought desperately to retain his image of Elijah Muhammed as a near-divinity despite growing awareness of the man's "immorality") to the probing, incredibly fluid "Malik" of his final days when he characterized himself as:

> I feel like a man who has been asleep somewhat and under someone else's control. I feel what I'm thinking and saying now is for myself. Before, it was for and by the guidance of Elijah Muhammad. Now I think with my own mind, sir.

The *Autobiography*, then, is legitimately an extended psychoanalytic interview, a record of transference, ambivalence and even to its most careful reader, countertransference.

—Cedric J. Robinson, "Malcolm Little as a Charismatic Leader," *Afro-American Studies* 3, No. 2 (September 1972): 87–88

[David P. Demarest, Jr., a professor of English at
Carnegie Mellon University, has edited *"The River Ran
Red": Homestead 1892* (1992). In this extract,
Demarest argues that *The Autobiography of Malcolm X*
is designed for black readers, but that non-blacks
should also read it if they wish to understand American
society.]

For many black readers, one ventures, *The Autobiography of
Malcolm X* will be a didactic experience. After all, Malcolm's
words are often clearly intended for a black audience, and
more often than not he is preaching and scolding blacks to
assert control over their own lives. Moreover, for most blacks
Malcolm's reputation will have preceded any reading of the
book, and they will be predisposed to see him as symbol of an
idea, to admire him for his reputation of standing up to whitey
and telling it loud and clear like it is—and challenging other
blacks to stand with him. As Ossie Davis puts it in his post-
script:

> . . . Malcolm kept snatching our lies away. He kept shouting the
> painful truths we whites and blacks did not want to hear from all
> the housetops. And he wouldn't stop for love nor money.

For blacks, *The Autobiography* will simply confirm and aug-
ment the general reputation to which Ossie Davis pays
homage—a reputation that has grown ever more vivid in the
black world since Malcolm's death. *The Autobiography* will
also reiterate many ideas that have been made familiar by black
militants. For black readers, Malcolm's fame will not rest on
personal knowledge of a book.

Whites—if they are to get beyond the fading memory of an
often harsh TV image—must read *The Autobiography*. And
unless they are indelibly biased or lack literary imagination,
they will become admirers of both Malcolm and the book.
Here, then, is a problem for the white critic. What makes *The
Autobiography* so effective with white readers? In part, the
appeal must involve ideology, though of a far more general-
ized sort than the advice applicable to the black community.

Certainly *The Autobiography* attracts white readers who feel that they too are exploited by the "system." But the white reader experiences *The Autobiography* as a *literary* work, and if he is converted to admiration of Malcolm, it is not simply because of ideology. He feels that he has been converted by something larger than and different from the ideas Malcolm specifically espouses—by something beyond didacticism.

Clearly *The Autobiography's* literary effectiveness is enhanced by some of its didactic aspects—its carefully symmetrical structure, for instance. Beginning at the beginning, Malcolm narrates his childhood and his teenage life of crime. Finally in prison, feeling that he has become Satan incarnate, he undergoes his first conversion, to Elijah Muhammad's religion. The chapter titled "Saved" is right at mid-point in the book— pages 169 through 190 in a total that runs to 382. After chronicling his activities in the Nation of Islam and his gradual estrangement from Elijah, Malcolm ends with his trip to Mecca and Africa and his conversion to a larger, more inter-racial faith. Such a schematic pattern might be expected of a didactic autobiographer who sees his life as moral exemplum and who seeks converts through advertisement of the road to wisdom that has been opened to him. Undeniably, *The Autobiography* gains a good deal of strength from the balanced clarity of this overall structure.

—David P. Demarest, Jr., "*The Autobiography of Malcolm X:* Beyond Didacticism," *CLA Journal* 16, No. 2 (December 1972): 179–80

PETER GOLDMAN ON MALCOLM X IN PRISON

[Peter Goldman (b. 1933) is a senior editor at *Newsweek*. He is the author of *Report from Black America* (1970) and the coauthor of *Charlie Company: What Viet Nam Did to Us* (1983) and *The Quest for the Presidency 1988* (1989). In this extract, Goldman dis-

cusses Malcolm X's days in prison and the early stages
of his conversion to Islam.]

Malcolm reformed in prison, or, rather, in spite of it. He served
seventy-seven months in three Massachusetts penitentiaries,
the first a stinking, century-old fortress at Charlestown with no
running water, no plumbing and no notion of rehabilitation
more advanced than keeping men locked in cells twenty hours a
day. Malcolm quickly discovered the local currency, cigarettes,
and what it could buy. "You can get anything in prison that you
can get in the streets if you know how to operate," he told an
interviewer once, and Malcolm, knowing how to operate, got
liquor, nutmeg, reefers, bennies and a dependably steady high.
The prison authorities typed him early on as "arrogant" and
"uncooperative," which seems rather to have understated the
case. Detroit Red, lately of the Apollo and the Savoy and
Small's Paradise Café, was known inside the walls as Satan—an
incorrigible hard-timer, with his mind, as he later put it, in a
"fog bag" and his gut in a state of permanent mutinous rage.

His rehabilitation was begun not by the penitentiary but by a
fellow impenitent, a convicted burglar called Bimbi whose
homemade education and gift of gab Malcolm noticed in the
yard and envied. Bimbi interested Malcolm in books and in
correspondence courses in English, Latin and German.
Malcolm was always, in surprising ways, deeply American,
even after his spiritual secession from us; being American, he
was pragmatic to the bone, and being a pragmatist, he saw
learning not as a pleasure or an end but as an instrument. At
first, it had no larger purpose for him than the little cachet it
gave him on the tier.

A purpose, and a calling, soon followed. I corresponded
briefly with Malcolm, after our meeting in St. Louis, and once
asked him how he had come into the Lost-Found Nation. It had
been—as Malcolm often told it—a classically Pauline conversion, a blinding, shattering transformation, only instead of a
flash of light and a vision of Jesus, there had been a nod of the
head from his kid brother Reginald and a glimpse of Satan.
Them. White people are the devil. Reginald, Malcolm wrote
me, had this on the authority of the Honorable Elijah
Muhammad, who learned it from Allah Himself, and he was

"able to convert me in five minutes. Despite my many experiences with whites, the fact that I had grown up with whites and was reared by whites and had socialized with whites in every form of their life, and even though I was in prison, I still respected whites. But when my brother told me that God had taught Mr. Elijah Muhammad that the white race was a race of Devils, my eyes came open on the spot."

Them. It was an authentic religious illumination, the innermost mystery of the Nation of the Lost-Founds, the first source of its authority over the faithful and its influence on countless blacks outside its immediate sway. Muslims and ex-Muslims I have met tend invariably to minimize the importance of the devil theory; white journalists have too often misunderstood it, have taken it as a personal affront rather than as an organizing principle akin in force, say, to the divinity of Christ or the labor theory of value. The faithful are therefore guarded when speaking about it to strangers. "People thought we were just talking about the white man is the devil," Benjamin Goodman told me. "No. It was men getting together and talking about everything—biology, chemistry, astronomy, world events, everything." The common formulation to outsiders is that the Muslims are not antiwhite but problack—that their first concern is to get black people to forget about whites and love themselves. This is surely true and yet only half the truth. For some part of black America, the possibility that white people are Satan incarnate has the force not only of religious metaphor but of empirical truth—a hypothesis by which one can at least explain why one lives in a rat-ridden slum and works, if at all, carrying the white man's baggage and diapering the white man's babies. It may be difficult to love oneself otherwise, given the circumstances of black life in America. A man may not be able to liberate himself from his condition by knowing who the devil is. But he may retrieve some part of his *amour-propre* if he understands how he got in that condition. He may even be able to recreate himself, as Malcolm did, so as no longer to pay the devil his dues.
—Peter Goldman, *The Death and Life of Malcolm X* (Urbana: University of Illinois Press, 1973), pp. 32–34

❧

[Paul John Eakin (b. 1938) is a professor of English at
Indiana University. He has written *Touching the World:
Reference in Autobiography* (1992) and edited
American Autobiography: Retrospect and Prospect
(1991). In this extract, Eakin studies Malcolm X's
changing view of autobiography from something static
to something fluid.]

In the final chapters of the *Autobiography* and in the
"Epilogue," as Malcolm X moves toward a new view of his
story as a life of changes, he expresses an impressive, highly
self-conscious awareness of the problems of autobiographical
narrative, and specifically of the complex relationship between
living a life and writing an autobiography. All of his experience
in the last packed months, weeks, and days of his life worked
to destroy his earlier confident belief in the completed self, the
completed life, and hence in the complete life story. Thus he
writes to Haley in what is possibly his final statement about the
Autobiography: "I just want to read it one more time because I
don't expect to read it in finished form." As Malcolm X saw it
at the last, all autobiographies are by nature incomplete and
they can not, accordingly, have a definitive shape. As a life
changes, so any sense of the shape of a life must change; the
autobiographical process evolves because it is part of the life,
and the identity of the autobiographical "I" changes and shifts.
Pursuing the logic of such speculations, Malcolm X even wonders whether any autobiography can keep abreast of the
unfolding of personal history: "How is it possible to write one's
autobiography in a world so fast-changing as this?" And so he
observes to Haley, "I hope the book is proceeding rapidly, for
events concerning my life happen so swiftly, much of what has
already been written can easily be outdated from month to
month. In life, nothing is permanent; not even life itself."

At the end, then, Malcolm X came to reject the traditional
autobiographical fiction that the life comes first, and then the
writing of the life; that the life is in some sense complete and
that the autobiographical process simply records the final

achieved shape. This fiction is based upon a suspension of time, as though the "life," the subject, could sit still long enough for the autobiographical "I," the photographer, to snap its picture. In fact, as Malcolm X was to learn, the "life" itself will not hold still; it changes, shifts position. And as for the autobiographical act, it requires much more than an instant of time to take the picture, to write the story. As the act of composition extends in time, so it enters the life-stream, and the fictive separation between life and life story, which is so convenient—even necessary—to the writing of autobiography, dissolves.

Malcolm X's final knowledge of the incompleteness of the self is what gives the last pages of the *Autobiography* together with the "Epilogue" their remarkable power: the vision of a man whose swiftly unfolding career has outstripped the possibilities of the traditional autobiography he had meant to write. It is not in the least surprising that Malcolm X's sobering insights into the limitations of autobiography are accompanied by an increasingly insistent desire to disengage himself from the ambitions of the autobiographical process. Thus he speaks of the *Autobiography* to Haley time and again as though, having disabused himself of any illusion that the narrative could keep pace with his life, he had consigned the book to its fate, casting it adrift as hopelessly obsolete. Paradoxically, nowhere does the book succeed, persuade, more than in its confession of failure as autobiography. This is the fascination of *The Education of Henry Adams,* and Malcolm X, like Adams, leaves behind him the husks of played-out autobiographical paradigms. The indomitable reality of the self transcends and exhausts the received shapes for a life that are transmitted by the culture, and yet the very process of discarding in itself works to structure an apparently shapeless experience. Despite—or because of—the intractability of life to form, the fiction of the completed self, which lies at the core of the autobiographical enterprise, cannot be readily dispatched. From its ashes, phoenix-like, it reconstitutes itself in a new guise. Malcolm X's work, and Adams' as well, generate a sense that the uncompromising commitment to the truth of one's own nature, which requires the elimination of false identities and careers one by one, will yield at the last the pure ore of a final and irreducible selfhood. This is the ultimate autobiographical dream.

—Paul John Eakin, "Malcolm X and the Limits of Autobiography," *Criticism* 18, No. 3 (Summer 1976): 241–42

STEPHEN J. WHITFIELD ON MALCOLM X'S CONTROL OF HIS IMAGE

[Stephen J. Whitfield (b. 1942), a professor of American studies at Brandeis University, is the author of *Into the Dark: Hannah Arendt and Totalitarianism* (1980), *A Critical American: The Politics of Dwight Macdonald* (1984), and *The Culture of the Cold War* (1991). In this extract, Whitfield examines Malcolm X's ability to control his image to the point that he became a lasting symbol of resistance and self-determination.]

One indication of how fully Malcolm X sensed that proper impressions must be engineered was his reaction to "the largest Hajj in history." Moved by the grandeur of his pilgrimage to Mecca, he regretted that "the Arabs are poor at understanding . . . the importance of public relations." He added that "Islam's conversions around the world could double and triple if the colorfulness . . . of the Hajj pilgrimage were properly advertised and communicated to the outside world." Unsatisfied with the Arabs' *insha Allah* ("God willing") and frustrated by the plodding recruitment practices of the Nation of Islam, he neatly turned one of Poor Richard's most familiar adages to his own ends: "I felt that Allah would be more inclined to help those who help themselves." One instance of self-help rather than trust in fate occurred when Detroit Red intimidated the other members of his burglary ring by playing Russian roulette. "I'm doing this, showing you I'm not afraid to die," he recalled telling them; and his objective was achieved: "They thought I was crazy. They were afraid of me." Yet according to the posthumous epilogue—but not the text itself—he told his amanuensis, Alex Haley: "I palmed the bullet. . . . Too many people would be so quick to say that's what I'm doing today, bluffing." No wonder. Labelled the only man in the country who could start or stop a race riot, he denied any interest in stopping one—yet during the ghetto conflagrations of the period he was elsewhere. Malcolm X refused to specify the seriousness of the power of Black Muslims by divulging membership figures, hinting only that those who knew weren't talking, those who were talking didn't know. He conceded the journalistic inflation of his influence; and it does not muffle the authentic cry of outrage and pain in his autobiography—undoubtedly composed with an eye cocked on posterity—to note how aptly Malcolm X learned the lesson imparted by his mentor Freddie in Boston: "The main thing you got to remember is that everything in the world is a hustle."

The mastery of impression management also included close attention to the symbolism of personal appearance. The rebellious colonies' ambassador to France chose not to hide his natural hair, and this supremely civilized man thus came across with a touch of the noble savage "among the powdered heads of Paris." The account of how Malcolm X got his first "long-haired, lye-cooked conk" is a grim ritual of self-degradation ending in his liberation as a Black Muslim and his self-acceptance, "with my natural kinky red hair." These testimonies to naturalness have a striking literary analogue in the apparent artlessness of their books, which lack the sublime sense of form and retrospective refinement that distinguish other classic autobiographies like Henry Adams' *Education* or Vladimir Nabokov's *Speak, Memory.* Neither nuance nor structure could be expected, with Franklin dashing off half—the more important half—of his memoir in about a week of rare leisure, in the form of a letter to his son; with Washington jotting down notes then ghosted into a coherent narrative by a white public relations man named Max Bennett Thrasher; and with Malcolm X not even writing his own recollections, but instead telling them during the coda of his life to a former Coast Guardsman.

—Stephen J. Whitfield, "Three Masters of Impression Management: Benjamin Franklin, Booker T. Washington, and Malcolm X as Autobiographers," *South Atlantic Quarterly* 77, No. 4 (Autumn 1978): 401–2

H. Porter Abbott on Malcolm X, St. Augustine, and the Nature of Autobiography

[H. Porter Abbott (b. 1940) is a professor of English at the University of California at Santa Barbara. He has written *The Fiction of Samuel Beckett: Form and Effect* (1973) and *Diary Fiction: Writing as Action* (1984). In this extract, Abbott compares the *Autobiography* to the *Confessions* of St. Augustine.]

The Autobiography of Malcolm X is a far cry from the austerity of Augustine's selective memory. Alex Haley, to whom Malcolm told his life, by his own account purposefully restrained Malcolm's desire to color the past with his present concerns, to fill it with praise of Allah and, later, denunciations of Elijah Muhammad. I would guess, too, that Haley may have, consciously or unconsciously, nursed from his subject that diversity of incident which the modern reader savours in a life—a legacy, in part, of Rousseau. Yet, particularly because it is an "as-told-to" autobiography, delivered, by Haley's account, in as unpremeditated and rambling a way as one could hope to find, it provides a good case study for the argument that organic form in the selected detail of a life, especially that of a convert, can arise without literary self-consciousness but rather from the spontaneous operation of the mind itself.

Malcolm, in fact, provides an instance of such an operation when he records the review of his life which he made during his conversion to the Muslim faith of Elijah Muhammad—the first of two religious conversions in his life and the one which dominates most of the personal record with which he provided Haley. Its immediate cause is the idea that the white man is the devil. In its unvarnished application, the idea allows Malcolm almost immediately to organize and understand his past through a selective recollection:

> The white people I had known marched before my mind's eye. From the start of my life. The state white people always in our house after the other whites I didn't know had killed my father . . . the white people who kept calling my mother "crazy" to her face and before me and my brothers and sisters, until she was finally taken off by white people to the Kalamazoo asylum . . . the white judge and others who had split up the

children . . . and the teachers—the one who told me in the eighth grade to "be a carpenter" because thinking of being a lawyer was foolish for a Negro.

In his Epilogue to *The Autobiography of Malcolm X,* Haley writes of the difficulty he had in getting Malcolm on the track of his childhood. Finally, exhausted by the continual polemic of his self-protective and untrusting subject, Haley, in an inspired moment, asked the simple question: "I wonder if you'd tell me something about your mother?" It turned out to be the key, and from that moment on Malcolm delivered in a kind of flood details from his life which, as he says, he had not thought about since they had happened.

The case might be made, I imagine, that Malcolm's mother played as important a role in the story of his conversion as St. Augustine's mother played in that of her son, but the attempt would involve a good deal of sheer speculation and ingenuity, given the material we have. It may also be that there is some underground connection between Malcolm's feeling for his mother and his extreme distrust of women. But, again, to make the case would require the recovery of details and a psychology which far exceed the text we have: in short, another life story. In this life story, the aspects of his mother which are allowed to emerge are allowed to do so precisely because of the powerfully teleological character of the life that is told—as it is conceived by the man who lived it.

> She was always standing over the stove, trying to stretch whatever we had to eat. We stayed so hungry that we were dizzy. I remember the color of dresses she used to wear—they were a kind of faded-out gray.

These are the first details of his life that Haley was permitted to know. They introduce the subject that dominates the first fourteen years of Malcolm's recalled life—the disintegration of his family—in which his mother was so central a figure by her efforts to keep the family together that she became a symbol both of the effort and the disintegration. Because of the converted awareness of the man who left prison in 1952, the long, painful deterioration that his memory organizes around his mother achieves its distinctive emphasis. For the destruction of the black family is now understood as a major instrument in the exertion of control by the white devil, a crime second only to the outright murder of black people (underscored at the outset of Malcolm's account by the killing of his black nationalist father), and a continual repetition in modern America of the original separation of fathers, mothers, sisters and brothers effected by the slave trade. By first destroying his strong, dominating father, white men had removed what little center of gravity the family had had. What was left was gradually eroded by want—itself a product of their earning power as black people—and white social workers who placed the children in separate families and finally had their mother declared mentally unbalanced and committed to an institution.

—H. Porter Abbott, "Organic Form in the Autobiography of a Convert: The Example of Malcolm X," CLA Journal 23, No. 2 (December 1979): 128–31

Gordon O. Taylor on Malcolm X and Change

[Gordon O. Taylor (b. 1938), a professor of English at the University of Tulsa, is the author of *Chapters of Experience: Studies in 20th Century American Autobiography* (1983) and *Studies in Modern American Autobiography* (1983). In this extract, Taylor notes the rapid and dramatic changes in Malcolm X's life that made the writing of his autobiography possible.]

"How is it possible to write one's autobiography in a world so fast-changing as this?" asks Malcolm X, in a letter quoted by Alex Haley in his epilogue to *The Autobiography of Malcolm X* (1965). The question is one asked implicitly by Henry Adams from first page to last of the *Education,* the outer world as ostensible subject having long since given way to demands of the inner, the autobiographical act compelled by the changes within and without which seem to prevent it. Change is for Malcolm X a matter of escalating tension between the idea of black life in America, as fixed in the design imposed by slavery, and a contrary notion, inseparable from the first, of possibilities achievable through black resistance to that design. This is essentially the double-consciousness Du Bois projects in *The Souls of Black Folk,* which gave Malcolm his first "glimpse into the black people's history before they came to this country." Under pressure of double-consciousness reminiscent of Wright, between narrowing lines of historical force, Malcolm's voice accelerates toward the end he foresees, creating in the process a self who survives before in fact destroyed. Considered in relation to the literary patterns surveyed above—of interplay between the written and the unwritten record, of the urge to articulate black self out of silence—the fact that the book was spoken to Haley is of secondary importance. *The Autobiography of Malcolm X* is what it has been called (here in Peter Goldman's words) by many, "a great American life, a compelling and irreplaceable book." The life violently ended (but no more violently, Malcolm argued before the fact, than the inner lives of black Americans continue to be lived) is now begun on a pilgrimage of text, which Haley makes clear is in its essence Malcolm's. The issue is finally one of readership as much as authorship, as Du Bois suggested in his plea to God the Reader that his book be truly heard. As Ellison's narrator says in *Invisible Man* (the words welling in the silence after "There's Many a Thousand Gone" is sung), "A whole unrecorded history is spoken then, . . . listen to what is said."

The story is told as Baldwin said it must be, compulsively, in symbols and signs, in hieroglyphics such as the cryptic notations Malcolm made on paper napkins Haley learned to leave near him during interviews. Malcolm X speaks from beyond his conversion to "the Lost-Found Nation of Islam here in this wilderness of North America," beyond also his break with Elijah Muhammad, a change in a "life of changes" moving him toward a core of constant self. He speaks at times from a sense of being "already dead," premonitions of assassination blending with the "whispered" rather than the documented truth of his father's lynching, with the historical fatality of his race's enslavement. Violence, as he puts it, "runs in my family." Such "posthumousness" of voice, recalling moments of similar sensibility in Baldwin, Wright, and Du Bois, is no less emotionally convincing for being a rhetorical pose. The making of the book is on one level a political act, like Malcolm's reenactment of his father's involvement in Marcus Garvey's "back to Africa" move- ment in his own commitment to the Muslim doctrine of separa- tion from white America. The personal progressively absorbs the political statement, however. He presents himself through- out as embodying the historical situation of "the black man in North America" (the equivalent but also the revision of "the Negro in America," the phrase in which Baldwin asserted his representative role), and the psychological tension collectively experienced by blacks.

Although the *Autobiography* contains no indication that he knew *Native Son,* in several passages Malcolm *is* Bigger, hold- ing within him the same prophecy of our future. He accepts (without limiting himself to) the role of "America's most dan- gerous and threatening black man, . . . the one who has been kept sealed up by the Northerner in the black ghetto." This type, like the conditions which create it, "needs no fuse; . . . it spontaneously combusts from within." Malcolm makes of him- self the archetypal "black prisoner," in whose ineradicable "memory of the bars" is also remembrance of the "first landing of the first slave ship." Such memory, from which historical identity has been erased, is itself the historical identity here reclaimed.

> —Gordon O. Taylor, "Voices from the Veil: Black American Autobiography," *Georgia Review* 35, No. 2 (Summer 1981): 354–55

CHARLES H. NICHOLS ON MALCOLM X'S INFLUENCE ON AMERICAN CULTURE

[Charles H. Nichols (b. 1919), formerly a professor of English at Brown University, edited *Many Thousands Gone: The Ex-Slaves' Account of Their Bondage* (1963) and *Arna Bontemps-Langston Hughes Letters* (1979). In this extract, Nichols argues that the *Autobiography* is the most widely read book in the black community and that it has changed the way people view race in America.]

The *Autobiography of Malcolm X* is probably the most influential book read by this generation of Afro-Americans. For not only is the account of Malcolm Little an absorbing and heart-shattering encounter with the realities of poverty, crime and racism. It is a fantastic success story. Paradoxically, the book designed to be an indictment of American and European bigotry and exploitation, is a triumphant affirmation of the possibilities of the human spirit. Malcolm X presents us with a manifesto, a call to arms, a revolutionary document. At the same time he reveals an incredible and dogged perseverance in the face of soul-destroying limitations, a passionate eagerness to learn, a love of life, an ingenious and resourceful capacity for survival. In him the picaresque mode is given a new psychic dimension, a sense of history and a tragic force. The chaos which would engulf the protagonist here extends in ever widening circles from the hunger, squalor and petty thievery of the street-corner to the crises in international relations and colonialism and, at last, to the vexed questions involving men's faith and their ultimate relation to the cosmos. The journey of the picaroon, Malcolm X, is from ragged obscurity to world spokesman, to charismatic leader, to martyred saint—a long, sordid, yet visionary, quest through the underworld to a vision of some just and ordered millennium. Thus the black picaresque characteristically presents us with the religious agonist whose search out of poverty, deprivation and despair leads him through dreams of liberation to a transcendent sense of community.

This then is the essential meaning of *The Autobiography of Malcolm X*. He was born into a family of eight children in Omaha, Nebraska on May 19, 1925. He knew poverty, hunger and deprivation. But above all his family lived surrounded by a ring of hate—constant threats by the Ku Klux Klan and innumerable forms of insult and indignity. Malcolm's father, a proud, militant man and Baptist preacher, propagated the Black Nationalism of Marcus Garvey. The bigots responded by burning down the Littles' house and, at last, murdering their father. Malcolm and his brothers were separated and farmed out to relatives and friends. His mother suffered a mental breakdown and had to be hospitalized. Malcolm was sent to Lansing, Michigan and then to Boston, Massachusetts. His schooling was sporadic.

The next phase of his life led him into petty crimes—truancy, thievery, dope peddling, pimping. Like the picaroon he survived by trickery and deceit, by out-smarting others, by "hustling" his way through a vicious underground existence. At last, apprehended by the police for one of his crimes, he landed in jail by the time he was sixteen or seventeen. Then came his conversion to the Black Muslim religion of Elijah Muhammad—a curious amalgam of myth, faith, asceticism and revolutionary doctrine. The Black Muslims' over-riding goal is the liberation of black people from the thralldom and exploitation of dominant white racists. They sought not only to prepare blacks for an inevitable confrontation with the power structure, but to give them a new self-esteem and pride and the determination to establish their own nation. The experience of conversion to the Muslim faith transformed Malcolm's character. Upon his release from prison, he turned from crime and self-indulgence to reading, learning and proselytizing for the group. His first exposure to the history of slavery, discrimination and imperialism convinced him that the "white man is a devil" and that black men must not only cast off the corrupting influence of western society, but work toward a separate black state, The Nation of Islam. One is amazed by Malcolm X's zeal for learning, by the range of his intellectual interests and the far-reaching character of his organizing effort for the cause. Malcolm listened as Elijah Muhammed railed against integration and reconciliation. He dedicated himself to the same cause and represented his great leader's ideas in innumerable speeches. Then came the break. Disillusioned by evidences of immorality and adultery charged against Elijah Muhammed, Malcolm X was silenced by the man who plainly felt threatened by his disciple's popularity. For Malcolm X understood the mentality of the ghetto—the stirrings and conflicts of the black masses. "The black man in North America was spiritually sick because for centuries he had accepted the white man's Christianity—which asked the black so-called Christian to expect no true Brotherhood of man but to endure the cruelties of the white so-called Christians. Christianity had made black men fuzzy, nebulous, confused in their thinking. . . ." he wrote. "The black man in North America was economically sick . . . as a consumer he got less than his share, and as a producer gave least . . . In New York City with over a million Negroes, there aren't twenty black-owned businesses employing over ten people. It's because black men don't own and control their own community's retail establishments that they can't stabilize their own community." These ideas got a wide hearing throughout the black world. The bitter disillusionment of the Negroes who had tried moral suasion, peaceful protest and non-violence only to confront dogs, clubs, guns and unjust imprisonment seized upon this new black nationalism. The assassination of Martin Luther King and Malcolm X himself changed radically the whole climate of race relations in America.

> —Charles H. Nichols, "The Slave Narrators and the Picaresque Mode: Archetypes for Modern Black Personae," *The Slave's Narrative*, ed. Charles T. Davis and Henry Louis Gates, Jr. (New York: Oxford University Press, 1985), pp. 289–91

SHIRLEY K. ROSE ON MALCOLM X'S ROAD TO LITERACY

[Shirley K. Rose is a professor of English and comparative literature at San Diego State University. In this extract, Rose explores the relationship between authorship and authenticity in the *Autobiography*, mapping Malcolm X's journey toward independence through education.]

The chronological organization allows readers to trace Malcolm X's development as a literate person from school child to internationally famous human rights activist. Each stage of his development can be marked by the name by which he was called or assumed for himself and later used to title each chapter of his narrative. Each change of name corresponds to a change of geographical place, representing the changing versions of reality in which and by which he explains the identities he creates for himself. While the changes of names are indications of changes in his developing sense of autonomy, the changes of place reflect the change of cultural groups in which he sought to participate. Together, these changes are represented in the narrative structure as a *pilgrimage*, a metaphor which becomes explicit near the end of his story, when he travels to Mecca. The difficulties he encounters on his quest for the sacred goal of autonomy are caused by his attempts to participate in the wrong communities—communities which limit who and what he can be.

The author first discusses learning to read and write in his account of his experiences at Mason Junior High School while he was living in a foster home. At this time, however, the actual acquisition of literacy skills is secondary to his socialization to the values of a literate society. Malcolm Little, the only black student in the class, was so popular among his classmates that he was asked to join numerous extracurricular organizations. But the acceptance he enjoyed was an acceptance based on his difference from his classmates, not on his equality with them.

Though he knew that as a black boy he was not a part of the white mainstream society, he believed in and accepted its myth that literacy and education gave one access to power, privilege, and autonomy. However, when he revealed his belief that the cultural myth could be extended to include him, that his literacy would give him power too, he learned that those who were part of the mainstream culture did not believe their reality included Malcolm Little.

The author chooses a telling incident to convey this lesson to his reader: When Mr. Ostrowski, his English teacher, asked Malcolm Little what he planned to do after he finished school and received the reply that he would like to be a lawyer, this teacher advised Malcolm to "be realistic . . . a lawyer—that's no realistic goal for a nigger." He suggested that instead Malcolm, the smartest student in his class, consider being a carpenter. Malcolm's response, to withdraw from his classmates, friends, and foster parents, was merely a manifestation of his recognition that the rewards which they expected for themselves were to be withheld from him.

The new identity which Malcolm assumed for himself when he left Michigan to live with his older half-sister, Ella, was that of a "Homeboy," the name given to him by his first friend in Boston. The author notes that this marked his real introduction to and immersion in black culture and the beginning of his street education, his socialization into a culture that would allow his participation. "Every day I listened raptly to customers who felt like talking, and it all added to my education. . . . I was thus schooled well" (83). His teachers were hustlers and criminals. The subjects were "the numbers, pimping, con games of many kinds, peddling dope, and thievery of all sorts, including armed robbery."

He pursued his new alternative education with all the intelligence and energy he was discouraged from devoting to an academic education. By his own account, his immersion in his street education led to success on the street. "Detroit Red" carried on a variety of hustles and other illegal activity until he was eventually imprisoned for robbery.

Once in prison he resumed, or rather began again, his acquisition of conventional literacy. His description of his "homemade education" during his seven years of imprisonment represents the myth of literacy as a path to autonomy. When his experience as a junior high school student had shown Malcolm X that this myth was not intended to be a part of the reality of a black person, he had substituted for it the success myth of the black ghetto. Later, as an inmate in the prison's white society had created for those who would not live by its laws, he responded by embracing the myth of literacy for autonomy and employing it against the cultural group from which he had learned it.

This myth also provides the plot for his account of his time in the Charlestown Prison, where "Satan" was first incarcerated. Here he began to read again in an effort to emulate a fellow inmate who was able to "command total respect . . . with his words." He began correspondence courses in the mechanics of English grammar and in Latin. Though he was aware of the usefulness of literacy skills, he was frustrated by his inability to read with comprehension. He says, "Pretty soon, I would have quit even these motions, unless I had received the motivation that I did."

He was motivated by a need for literacy skills in order to carry on a correspondence with his brothers and sisters as well as with the Black Muslim prophet Elijah Muhammad. Through this correspondence he found a way to fight against white society for his human rights. The correspondence began with that first one-page letter which he wrote at least twenty-five times, trying to make it legible and understandable. He describes his skills at this time: "I practically couldn't read my handwriting myself; it shames even to remember it. My spelling and my grammar were as bad, if not worse."

He did not let the frustration stop him, but instead practiced the literacy skills repeatedly until, eventually, he was not only writing a letter a day to Elijah Mohammad and a letter a day to one or another of his brothers and sisters, but was also writing to the people he had known on the streets in Harlem. His sense that this practice of literacy was changing him, that he was becoming a literate person, is reflected in his remark that the hustlers to whom he wrote were "too uneducated to write a letter . . . privately, they would get someone else to read a letter if they received one."

His awareness of himself as literate led to a growing confidence that he could use his literacy to bring about further changes in his life. The unique program of study he describes—copying from the dictionary "to study, to learn some words . . . to improve my penmanship"—was totally self-motivated and it was effective. He could "for the first time pick up a book and read and now begin to understand what the book was saying." To describe the effect of this new awareness of his literacy, he uses such expressions as "a new world that opened" and claims "I had never been so truly free in my life."
—Shirley K. Rose, "Metaphors and Myths of Cross-Cultural Literacy: Autobiographical Narratives by Maxine Hong Kingston, Richard Rodriguez, and Malcolm X," *MELUS* 14, No. 1 (Spring 1987): 5–7

[Robert Michael Franklin (b. 1954) is a professor of ethics and society at Emory University and the director of Black Church Studies. He is the author of *Liberating Visions: Human Fulfillment and Social Justice in African-American Thought* (1990), from which the following extract is taken. Here, Franklin explores Malcolm X's introduction to the Nation of Islam and its significance in his life.]

Both during and after his years in the Nation of Islam, Malcolm believed profoundly that Islam was the only religious system capable of providing firm, practical rules for moral living and high self-esteem for struggling blacks. He believed that Islam was able to generate the "moral reformation necessary to up the level of the so-called Negro community by eliminating the vices and the other evils that destroy the moral fiber of the community." Often the purist, Malcolm considered personal moral integrity (purity and honesty) to be a prerequisite for leadership and participation in civilized society. Like Du Bois, he charged that Christianity had failed to instill in blacks a pride in their culture, history, and identity. It had instead taught blacks to aspire to white American and European values. It had become an oppressive faith.

For Malcolm and thousands of other young blacks, Elijah Muhammad's version of Islam contained a deconstructive function. Blacks needed some alternative to the "white American Christianity" that enslaved them psychologically. Equipped with a liberating faith, they would be able to love themselves and their fellows and be empowered to transform an unjust society.

> I feel the responsibility . . . to help you comprehend for the first time what this white man's religion that we call Christianity has done to us.
> I know you didn't expect this. Because almost none of us black people have thought that maybe we were making a mistake not wondering if there wasn't a special religion somewhere for us—*a special religion for the black man.*
> Well, there is such a religion. It's called Islam. But I'm going to tell you about Islam a little later. First, we need to understand

some things about this Christianity before we can understand why the answer for us is Islam. (Italics mine.)

Malcolm's diagnosis went beyond merely scolding the oppressed for absorbing the oppressor's religion to confronting them with the logical question of why they had not considered the existence of a religion especially suitable for their situation. Blacks were victims of a propaganda effort to socialize them into becoming innocuous Christians before they discovered sacred worldviews that allowed, even encouraged, revolution in the name of God.

Following his hajj to Mecca, Malcolm received his "new insight into the true religion of Islam." Thereafter, he articulated a more socially integrative and constructive role for Islam in pluralistic America. He observed, "America needs to understand Islam, because this is the one religion that erases from its society the race problem." "True Islam removes racism, because people of all colors and races who accept its religious principles and bow down to the one God Allah, also automatically accept each other as brothers and sisters, regardless of differences in complexion." The religion of Islam eradicated personal behaviors and attitudes that prevented individual fulfillment and removed the social barriers to multiracial community to make communal fulfillment possible. Whatever other roles religion might serve for humanity, for oppressed people, its primary task entailed the reconstruction of black self-hood, which had been fragmented by the traumas of oppression.

In the first phase of Malcolm's posthustler life, Muhammad's interpretation of Islam helped to liberate Malcolm from vices of the flesh: in his post–Nation of Islam days, orthodox Islam liberated him from vices of the spirit. In the Nation of Islam, blacks were portrayed as the "original race" who created civilization and disseminated knowledge. This suited Malcolm's need for self-esteem for over a decade, but the pilgrimage quickened the pace of his disillusionment with a narrow, sectarian faith. In his brief encounter with orthodox Islam, he discovered the basis for a rational, universal, morally effective liberating faith. Malcolm acknowledged the value of both "moments" of his Islamic faith journey and chose not to disparage Muhammad's ministry among the black underclass.

Nevertheless, secretly he knew that this form of faith was only a partial liberation. Ultimately, all blacks should discover their highest identity and loyalties in the universal family of God. He believed orthodox Islam could facilitate this step.

> —Robert Michael Franklin, *Liberating Visions: Human Fulfillment and Social Justice in African-American Thought* (Minneapolis: Fortress Press, 1990), pp. 91–93

HENRY LOUIS GATES, JR. ON SPIKE LEE AND THE *AUTOBIOGRAPHY*

[Henry Louis Gates, Jr. (b. 1950), one of the leading scholars of black American literature, is the W. E. B. Du Bois Professor of Humanities at Harvard University. Among his many books are *The Signifying Monkey: A Theory of Afro-American Literary Criticism* (1988), *Loose Canons: Notes on the Culture Wars* (1992), and *Colored People: A Memoir* (1994). In this extract, Gates celebrates the new interest in *The Autobiography of Malcolm X* produced by Spike Lee's film.]

One of the most gratifying effects of Spike Lee's film "Malcolm X" is that its success has prompted the restoration of Malcolm's autobiography to the best-seller lists. The country is *reading* the 1965 book once again, as avidly, it seems, as it is seeing Mr. Lee's movie. For 17 weeks *The Autobiography of Malcolm X,* written with the assistance of Alex Haley, has been on the New York Times paperback best-seller list, and for 10 of those weeks it was No. 1. Today, on the 28th anniversary of his assassination, Malcolm's story has become as American—to borrow H. Rap Brown's famous aphorism—as violence and cherry pie. ⟨. . .⟩

I loved the hilarious scene in which Malcolm is having his hair "conked," or "processed" ("relaxed" remains the euphemism); unable to rinse out the burning lye because the pipes in his home are frozen, he has no recourse but to dunk his head in a toilet bowl. A few months before, the benignly parochial principal of our high school had "paddled" my schoolmate Arthur Galloway when Arthur told him that his processed hairstyle was produced by a mixture of eggs, mashed potatoes and lye. "Don't lie to me, boy," the principal was heard saying above Arthur's protests.

What I remember most, though, is Malcolm's discussion of the word "aardvark":

"I saw that the best thing I could do was get hold of a dictionary—to study. . . . I spent two days just riffling uncertainly through the dictionary's pages. I'd never realized so many words existed! . . . Funny thing, from the dictionary first page right now, that 'aardvark' springs to my mind. The dictionary had a picture of it, a long-tailed, long-eared, burrowing African mammal, which lives off termites caught by sticking out its tongue as an anteater does for ants."

Years later, near the end of his life, Malcolm found himself heading to the American Museum of Natural History in New York to learn more about that exotic creature, even while trying to figure out how to avoid an almost certain Muslim death sentence. "Boy! I never will forget that old aardvark!" he had mused to Alex Haley. What manner of politician was this, I wondered, in this the year that Stokely Carmichael and Rap Brown, Eldridge Cleaver and Huey P. Newton, Ron Karenga and Amiri Baraka, simultaneously declared themselves to be the legitimate sons of Malcolm the father, to linger with aardvarks when his world was collapsing around him?
—Henry Louis Gates, Jr., "Malcolm, the Aardvark and Me," *New York Times Book Review,* 21 February 1993, p. 11

DANIEL KEMPTON ON MALCOLM X AS AUTODIDACT

[Daniel Kempton, a professor of political science at Northern Illinois University, is the author of *Soviet*

Strategy toward Southern Africa: The National Liberation Movement Connection (1989). In this extract, Kempton explores Malcolm X's long struggle to educate himself and some of its results.]

The story Malcolm X tells of his "homemade education" is a narrative of salvation and deliverance, of success against formidable odds which make the ordinary difficulties of education seem trivial in comparison. The epithet "homemade" underscores the struggle involved, but it also evokes the ideal of education as *self-instruction* (as opposed to indoctrination), instruction that begins and ends "at home," in the self. His story shows our freshmen the liberatory power of writing—as a technical instrument for conveying ideas, as an agent of social criticism and intervention, as an expressive medium in which to fashion the self—and it holds out the promise that this power is theirs to command, if only they apply themselves with diligence to the fundamentals of composition, mastering one word at a time. There is also a cautionary lesson: if they do *not* master writing and become "functional," then writing will master them. The illiterate person does not know his (her) own true identity because she (he) has been named by the discourse of some Other. Given the nature of our political life, this discourse is bound to be interested, and it may furthermore be oppressive; Malcolm X would say that it is inevitably so— "whitened." It is not now unusual for composition textbooks and freshman readers to devote a good deal of attention to the issue of oppression through language: problems such as inveterate racism and sexism in language or the deliberate manipulation of language in propaganda and advertising. And like Malcolm X, the textbooks propose as the corrective to these linguistic and *social* problems the ideal of an authentic writing—writing that is honest, clear, rational, correct. This is a classic humanist project, which has been defined for more than one generation of teachers and students by George Orwell's often-anthologized essay of 1946 on politics and language: "Modern English, especially written English, is full of bad habits . . . which can be avoided if one is willing to take the necessary trouble. If one gets rid of these habits one can think more clearly, and to think more clearly is a necessary first step toward political regeneration: so that the fight against bad English is not frivolous and is not the exclusive concern of professional writers." The fight against ideologically charged discourse, the bad English written in modern times, is the legitimate concern of every American citizen, since, as Malcolm X impresses upon us, the country stands desperately in need of political regeneration. The principal weapon for this fight is the writer's most basic resource—the dictionary.

—Daniel Kempton, "Writing the Dictionary: The Education of Malcolm X," *Centennial Review* 37, No. 2 (Spring 1993): 259–60

MICHAEL ERIC DYSON ON THE STRUCTURE OF THE *AUTOBIOGRAPHY*

[Michael Eric Dyson, a professor of religion at Harvard Divinity School, is the author of *Reflecting Black: African American Cultural Criticism* (1993). In this extract from his book on Malcolm X, Dyson discusses the structure of the *Autobiography,* arguing that it is as much the product of Alex Haley's literary talents as of Malcolm's retelling of his own story.]

The tripartite division of the life follows faithfully the lineaments of Malcolm's various emergences and conversions as detailed in his autobiography (as told to Alex Haley), *The Autobiography of Malcolm X.* That text itself has been criticized for avoiding or distorting certain facts. Indeed, the autobiography is as much a testament to Haley's ingenuity in shaping the manuscript as it is a record of Malcolm's own attempt to tell his story. The profound personal, intellectual, and ideological changes Malcolm was undergoing near the end of his life led him to order the events of his life to support a mythology of metamorphosis and transformation that bore fruit in spiritual wisdom. But that document bears deep traces as well of Malcolm's attempt to fend against the inevitable vulnerabilities revealed in the process of recalling and reconstructing one's life. In simple terms, this means that Malcolm's claim that he was expelled from West Junior High School in Lansing, Michigan, for instance, is inaccurate; he slid through the seventh grade there in 1939. In a more profound manner, however, Malcolm never mentions his meeting with the Ku Klux Klan in 1961 to see if that group, which like the Nation of Islam espoused racial separatism, could help Elijah Muhammad and his followers obtain land to implement their beliefs.

As with most autobiographies, Malcolm's recollections were an effort to impose order on the fragments of his experience. The story of his escape from functional illiteracy, his exodus from mental and social slavery, and his conversion to true belief—only to have that belief betrayed by the father figure of his faith—is a narrative whose philosophical pedigree draws on Augustine, Booker T. Washington, Frederick Douglass, and Sigmund Freud. To the extent that Lee embellishes the historical account, he is being faithful in a way to the spirit of self–re-creation that Malcolm evidenced in his colorful telling of his own life.

—Michael Eric Dyson, *Making Malcolm: The Myth and Meaning of Malcolm X* (New York: Oxford University Press, 1995), pp. 134–35

Books by
Malcolm X

Malcolm X Speaks: Selected Speeches and Statements.
   Ed. George Breitman. 1965.

Two Speeches. 1965.

The Autobiography of Malcolm X (with Alex Haley). 1965.

The Speeches of Malcolm X at Harvard. Ed. Archie Epps. 1968.

Malcolm X Talks to Young People. 1969.

By Any Means Necessary: Speeches, Interviews, and a Letter.
   Ed. George Breitman. 1970.

The End of White World Supremacy: Four Speeches.
   Ed. Benjamin Goodman. 1971.

The Last Speeches. Ed. Bruce Perry. 1989.

*Malcolm X Talks to Young People: Speeches in the U.S., Britain,
   and Africa.* 1991.

Malcolm X Speaks Out. Ed. Nan Richardson, Catherine
   Chermayeff, and Antoinette White. 1992.

February 1965: The Final Speeches. 1992.

The Black Book of Malcolm X. Ed. Nan Richardson and
   Catherine Chermayeff. 1992.

Books by
Alex Haley

The Autobiography of Malcolm X (with Malcolm X). 1965.

Roots. 1976.

A Different Kind of Christmas. 1988.

The Playboy *Interviews.* 1993.

Alex Haley's Queen: The Story of an African Family
(with David Stevens). 1993.

Books about
Malcolm X, Alex Haley, and
The Autobiography of
Malcolm X

Asante, Molefi Kete. *Malcolm X as Cultural Hero and Other Afrocentric Essays.* Trenton, NJ: Africa World Press, 1993.

Benson, Thomas W. "Rhetoric and Autobiography: The Case of Malcolm X." *Quarterly Journal of Speech* 60 (1974): 1–13.

Berthoff, Werner. "Witness and Testament: Two Contemporary Classics." *New Literary History* 2 (1970–71): 311–27.

Breitman, George. *The Last Year of Malcolm X: The Evolution of a Revolutionary.* New York: Pathfinder Press, 1967.

Carew, Jan R. *Ghosts in Our Blood: With Malcolm X in Africa, England, and the Caribbean.* New York: Lawrence Hill Books, 1994.

Carson, Clayborne. *Malcolm X: The FBI File.* New York: Carroll & Graf, 1991.

Clark, Kenneth B. *The Negro Protest: James Baldwin, Malcolm X, Martin Luther King Talk with Kenneth B. Clark.* Boston: Beacon Press, 1963.

Dyson, Michael Eric. "Who Speaks for Malcolm X? The Writings of Just About Everybody." *New York Times Book Review,* 29 November 1992, pp. 3, 29, 31, 33.

Ferris, William. "The Hummingbird: An Interview with Alex Haley." *Crossroads* 1, No. 2 (Spring–Summer 1993): 1–10.

Gallen, David. *Malcolm X: As They Knew Him.* New York: Carroll & Graf, 1992.

Gianakos, Perry E. "The Black Muslims: An American Millennialistic Response to Racism and Cultural Deracination." *Centennial Review* 23 (1979): 430–51.

Groppe, John D. "From Chaos to Cosmos: The Role of Trust in *The Autobiography of Malcolm X*." *Soundings* 66 (1983): 437–49.

Harper, Frederick D. "A Reconstruction of Malcolm X's Personality." *Afro-American Studies* 3 (1972): 1–6.

Henry, Joseph. "The Public, Spiritual, and Humanistic Odyssey of Malcolm X: A Critical Bibliographical Debate." *Iowa Journal of Literary Studies* 4 (1983): 77–93.

Hentoff, Nat. "Finding Malcolm X." *Yale Review* 76 (1986–87): 181–83.

Jamal, Hakim A. *From the Dead Level: Malcolm X and Me.* London: Andre Deutsch, 1971.

Karim, Benjamin, et al. *Remembering Malcolm.* New York: Carroll & Graf, 1992.

Lee, Spike, and Ralph Wiley. *By Any Means Necessary: The Trials and Tribulations of the Making of* Malcolm X. New York: Hyperion, 1992.

Leigh, David J. "Malcolm X and the Black Muslim Search for Ultimate Reality." *Ultimate Reality and Meaning* 13 (1990): 33–49.

Perry, Bruce. *Malcolm: The Life of a Man Who Changed Black America.* Barrytown, NY: Station Hill Press, 1991.

Rajiv, Sudhi. *Forms of Black Consciousness.* New York: Advent, 1992.

Rich, Andrea L., and Arthur L. Smith. *Rhetoric of Revolution: Samuel Adams, Emma Goldman, Malcolm X.* Durham, NC: Moore Publishing Co., 1970.

Sales, William W. *From Civil Rights to Black Liberation: Malcolm X and the Organization of Afro-American Unity.* Boston: South End Press, 1994.

Seraile, William. "David Walker and Malcolm X: Brothers in Radical Thought." *Black World* 22, No. 12 (October 1973): 68–73.

Stone, Albert E. "Collaboration in Contemporary Autobiography." *Revue Française d'Etudes Américaines* No. 14 (May 1982): 151–65.

Strickland, William. *Malcolm X: Make It Plain.* New York: Viking, 1994.

Terry, Eugene. "Black Autobiography: Discernible Forms." *Okike* 19 (September 1981): 6–10.

Weiss, Samuel A. "The Ordeal of Malcolm X." *South Atlantic Quarterly* 77 (1978): 497–507.

Wolfenstein, E. Victor. *The Victims of Democracy: Malcolm X and the Black Revolution.* Berkeley: University of California Press, 1981.

Index of
Themes and Ideas